NAVIAN LIBRARY

R. Graubard (ed.)	Norden – The Passion for Equality
. Dahl	Democracy, Liberty, and Equality
)sterud (ed.)	Studies of War and Peace
enstadt	European Civilization in a Comparative Perspective
ng Dahl	Women's Law
aria Hernes	Welfare State and Woman Power
E. Lindblom	Democracy and Market System
erberg	Metasociology
Aubert	Continuity and Development
sson (ed.)	Generating Equality in the Welfare State
ne Stølen and Vaa (eds)	Gender and Change in Developing Countries
Gullestad	The Art of Social Relations: Essays on Culture, Social Action and Everyday Life in Modern Norway
dhaug	The Shadow Educational System
ngaard (ed.)	Parliamentary Change in the Nordic Countries
P. Boje and)lsson-Hort (eds)	Scandinavia in a New Europe

SCAND

Stephen

Robert

Øyvind

S. N. Ei

Tove St

Helga M

Charles

Dag Ös

Vilhelm

Inga Pe

Kristi A
Mariken

Mariann

Odd No

Erik Da

Thomas
Sven E.

Birth Law

Edited by
Anne Hellum

SCANDINAVIAN
UNIVERSITY PRESS

Scandinavian University Press (Universitetsforlaget AS),
0608 Oslo, Norway
Distributed world-wide excluding Norway by
Oxford University Press, Walton Street, Oxford OX2 6DP

Oxford New York Toronto Dehli Bombay Calcutta Madras
Karachi Kuala Lumpur Singapore Hong Kong Tokyo Nairobi
Dar es Salaam Cape Town Melbourne Auckland Madrid
and associated companies in Berlin Ibadan

Oxford is a trade mark of Oxford University Press

Published in the United States by
Oxford University Press Inc., New York

ISBN 82-00-21286-6

Published with grants from NORAD (Norwegian Agency for Development Cooperation) and The Royal Norwegian Ministry of Foreign Affairs

British Library Cataloguing in Publication Data
Data available

Library of Congress Cataloguing in Publication Data
Data available

Printed in Norway by
A/S Foto-Trykk, Trøgstad 1993

Contents

Acknowledgements

This book comprises a collection of articles on the subject of birth law which have been written by researchers at the Institute of Women's Law at the Faculty of Law in Oslo during the course of the last ten years. In 1977, with her student thesis, "Birth Law and Equality", Marianne Fastvold lay the conceptual foundation for the systematic development of the birth process as a legal field. The aim behind the anthology is to make available to an international public knowledge of some of the perspectives which have been developed within Norwegian women's law, and birth law in particular.

During recent years, women's law has become increasingly more global and comparative in nature, and within the context of this internationalization, birth law has occupied a central position. The original impetus for the anthology was the wide cooperation which since 1987 has existed between Norwegian and African women's law researchers through the NORAD Diploma Course in Women's Law for Lawyers from Southern and Eastern Africa. The factual and legal aspects of the processes of birth and fertility have played a central role within this international and cross-cultural cooperation.

Some of the articles in the anthology have been financed under the NORAS programme on equality research. NORAD and the Norwegian Ministry for Foreign Affairs have contributed financially towards translation of the articles, which has been undertaken by Ronald Walford and Mary Bjærum. Jane Wesenberg has undertaken linguistic revision of the translated texts. Sissel Waage, Anne Lene Svingen and Mette Rygsæter have assisted with proofreading and the bibliography.

My warm thanks go to Professor Tove Stang Dahl who, in the conception and development of birth law, has been of great inspiration to all of the contributors to this anthology.

Oslo, 6 January 1993

Anne Hellum

1

Equal Status and Birth Law*

TOVE STANG DAHL

I. To What Do We Give Equal Status?

Equal status favours manliness. The equal status policy has its qualitative basis in male life contexts as guiding norms for the organization of society, and the result of equal status is measured by counting heads with male and female bodies. To put it simply, the objective has been an approximately equal distribution of male and female heads in as many contexts as possible, but with an over-emphasis on the contexts in which men operate, and on the rights and duties – but especially the rights – consequent upon participation in these contexts.

This introduction of more women into men's areas leads in many respects to an improvement in and perhaps a liberation of women's situation in life. But women's life contexts become at the same time more strongly linked to men's, leaving correspondingly less room for traditional female self-expression, activities, and values. The total composite result of equal status may, paradoxically enough, be a reinforcement of the male norms, i.e. the already prevailing cultural hegemony, to the disadvantage of the already hard-pressed female life values.

The Equal Status Act: The Life of a Wage-earner Before Family Life.

The Act relating to Equal Status between the Sexes of 1978 is a good public law example of the application of a male norm to the organization of the sexes.

The Act is intended to promote equal status between the sexes and is specially designed to improve the status of women (s.1). An interesting factor to note, however, is that the objects clause of the Norwegian Act is gender specific, as opposed to legislation in other countries which is gender neutral. Thc provision to the effect that *women are to be given formal precedence* over men was introduced late in the legislative process, after the gender-neutral form of the first bill was strongly criticized by parts of the women's movement.

The women's movement demonstrated how a gender-neutral equal status Act could easily have directly harmful consequences for the weaker sex.

Thus, at a time when legislation relating to all sectors of societal life was being systematically scrutinized in order to render it as gender-neutral as possible, a new gender-specific provision was enacted in Norway. This was remarkable in itself, but correct. The system adopted by the Act is that women as a group (or special groups of women) shall be given priority over men in the general application of the equal status policy. Moreover, individual women can take advantage of the provision by interpretation of the Act in individual cases. From this point of view the Equal Status Act is an enactment favourable to women and a step on the way to a "woman-friendly State" (Hernes 1987).

I have therefore no objections against the premises of the Act. The objects clause, on its own, is a female norm, which is to be given precedence if it conflicts with a male norm. The problem lies in the material and procedural applications of the Act with regard to *how* the sexes shall be more equal – in what areas and to what extent. In both these contexts it is a male norm which is applied, both with regard to material content and procedural enforcement, as will appear below. It is manliness that is accorded equal status, not womanliness.

The public authorities are bound to make proper arrangements for equal status between the sexes in *all* areas of society, but the objects clause specifies that "women and men shall be given equal opportunities for education, work and cultural and professional development" (s.1(2) and (3)). The areas that are specified, thereby revealing the main applications of the Act, are traditionally male areas. The traditionally male life contexts are further emphasized, partly through the specifications and partly through the exceptions made in the subsequent provisions.

Equal status in the case of employment (s.4), equal pay for work of equal value (s.5), equal right to education (s.6), and equal opportunity in all forms of association (s.8) are all subject to special regulation. It is in respect to these areas that we find ourselves at the core of the Act: primarily the paid-work market, secondly the educational system and policy. This core is further emphasized by the enforcement provisions of the Act, where particular consideration has been paid to avoid conflict between the Equal Status Act and the interests of industrial organizations. If an equal status case *indirectly* raises questions concerning the validity, interpretation, or continued existence of a wage agreement, the parties to the said agreement can elect to have the case decided by the Labour Disputes Court instead of by the Equal Status Appeals Board, cf. s.14(1). And, as is reasonable, the Board cannot decide upon matters which, according to labour law legislation, *come under the jurisdiction of the Labour Disputes Court*, cf. s.14(2). The male interests of organized industry were altogether well taken care of through lobbying during the preparatory work on the Act (Skjeie 1982).

If we examine the exemption provisions of the Act, the picture becomes clearer. Firstly, an absolute exemption is made for internal relations in religious communities. In these communities it is men who rule, but freedom of religion is accorded natural precedence over the Equal Status Act s.2(1). In our context, however, the second paragraph of this provision must be specially emphasized: "In respect of family life and purely personal relationships", the Act shall not be enforced by the equal status authorities.

One can see how the Act operates by enforcing a male norm, even though female life contexts fall within the scope of the Act. Within the nucleus of the Act, women shall be assisted or protected in certain male life contexts – be given the opportunity to become more like men – at any rate as long as they do not directly cross strong interests in industrial life. But the Act does not arrange for men to be guided into female life contexts, since central contexts such as family life are only given a place in the penumbra of the Act.

If a married woman wishes to take legal action under the Equal Status Act in order to establish her husband's obligation to take part also in the support in kind of the family (and not only or primarily the financial support), she must resort to the ordinary law courts and not to the equal status authorities. It is complicated enough if in family life and other personal relations one applies to the authorities to solve conflicts – the personal relations are then probably already close to dissolution. But it is far more complicated to bring an action in the law courts than to raise the issue with the Equal Status Commissioner or Board.

It is not, however, my opinion that the complete inclusion of family life in the Equal Status Act would make it a useful instrument in personal distributions of rights and duties. But in law the basic principles are important. The Act also has symbolic and ideological functions. It is therefore in my opinion not unimportant to discuss the relative ranking of wage-earner life and family life in the Equal Status Act.

A strengthening of the position of family life in the Equal Status Act may also have effects in *other* contexts than relations between the parties to family life, e.g. by maintaining an unemployed father's right to be accepted as a local employment seeker by the social security authorities, on an equal footing with the mother – because of his equal duties of care according to the Children Act of 1981.

The Wage-earner State

The present ranking of wage-earner life and family life in the Equal Status Act will no doubt enable more women to seek and take paid employment, and thereby help to improve women's situation as regards the right to money and a wider working environment. But at the same time, paid work is reinforced as a social institution by the fact that more women are led towards greater equality with men, without their actually achieving occupational and financial equality, and without the occurrence of a corresponding movement of men in the direction of greater efforts in the unpaid female life contexts. The *family* is weakened. Paradoxically enough, an improvement in women's situation in the paid work sector leads at the same time to a further societal subordination of women's life to men's.

The women who live as much like men as possible, who acquire an education and use it in incessant and career-orientated work in the market, are also the women who get the best return, not only in regular income but also in social security.

As regards grants of benefits pursuant to the National Insurance Act of 1966, this circumstance is striking. The Norwegian welfare state is mainly a wage-earner state, created through market interests and compromises between the participants (Dahl 1990a). The special female life contexts also have their place in the wage-earner state, but more in the way which men have perceived them than in the way women have demanded them. The rules for distribution of social rights have been laid down in what Tone Sverdrup calls *the dual-track legal system*, based on a male model and a female model in legal policy. Women have been objects rather than subjects in legal development, which means that women have throughout been left behind or totally excluded as regards legal rights.[1] We do not give womanliness equal status. We have without doubt begun to note the somewhat increased time spent by men in family and care work and to study the development in men's supporter role (Widerberg 1985); likewise how many – or rather, how few – fathers exercise their statutory birth and care rights pursuant to the Working Environment Act and the National Insurance Act (Widerberg 1984, Ketscher 1986, Kaul 1990); or men's interest in using the Children Act of 1981 to obtain custody of the children of the family following a divorce (Sandberg 1990, Smith 1980). But these trends are not the main point if one wishes to give womanliness equal status with manliness. In such an equal status strategy, it is *the female life contexts* which must be strengthened and given legal rights in themselves, whether these are exercised by women or by men. On these bases it is *a female norm* that must be established and reinforced on a par with the male life contexts. And in forming such a strategy, it is natural to take as a starting point the need for research into and a policy concerning birth.

II. Birth as a Common and Special Experience

From a woman's standpoint, it is natural in a double sense – both biologically and socially – to develop a philosophy and policy concerning birth. After studying the works of the foremost thinkers, Mary O'Brien points out that there is no philosophy concerning birth to be found in the male tradition, such as one finds concerning other natural functions and biological necessities, such as food, sexuality and death. Birth is not a process that the male tradition has found interesting, either ontologically or epistemologically at the biological level. It is the human family that has been of philosophical interest, while its biological basis is simply taken for granted (O'Brien 1981).

This is not really so surprising. Men have what Unni Wikan calls a *close-experience* relationship to food, sexuality and death, but a more distant and sporadic relationship to birth. The *result* of sexuality – the relationship to mother and child – is, however, a strong close-experience for men. It is therefore natural that these relations have been set down in philosophy and legal provisions concerning the patriarchal family.

Contributions from women's philosophy are awaited with special interest in this area. Personal experience leaves its mark not only on what philosophers and other researchers are interested in but also on what they think and are capable of thinking (Wikan 1989).

As human beings we all have a common experience in birth. But in one's life, one's own birth is pushed into the background, only to emerge perhaps in extreme existential situations later on, e.g. through a new birth or death. Stanislav Grof has made interesting studies of people close to death, in existential crises, intoxication or ecstasy (with reproductions of experiences from all corners of the world and from his own therapeutic activity using LSD on the chronically ill and the dying). When mountaineers fall they are capable of re-experiencing their own birth; and under LSD intoxication both patient and therapist can wander in the fields of creation (Grof 1979).

A common experience for women who give birth is the thought that "never have I been so fully alive and yet so close to death at the same time". This cognition is deepened in the case of subsequent births, and it represents perhaps the deepest femaleness: a way of understanding that recognizes that in life death is present, and in death life; in the procreation of one thing lies also the dissolution of others, and in this dissolution one rejoices that something is generated.

When I allow myself to characterize this way of experiencing and thinking as "the deepest femaleness", it is not, of course, my intention to exclude men from experiential thinking of a similar kind. I have in fact myself often encountered it in male artists. What I wish to emphasize is that women *of necessity* – through an urge, but also sometimes quite involuntarily – become involved in birth and care relations which also at the general level seem to generate such a way of understanding. This way of understanding is created by an interplay between women's direct personal experiences and the inheritance of women's culture which occurs in the learning process between the generations (Chodorow 1978, Gilligan 1982). A *"circular" and relational way of understanding*, from a philosophical point of view, thus seems to be more natural for women on the basis of women's personal experiences than it is for men.

Modern women's research has from the very first pointed out that the male – and therefore the scientific – way of thinking employs dualisms and dichotomies instead of relational reasoning. Dualisms are often used as tools to demonstrate and analyse qualities, values and relationships which lie separate from each other, each on its own linear scale, in either gliding temporal or hierarchical transitions; or separated by their oppositional nature, not infrequently either/or relationships, possibly dialectical relationships: e.g. spirit/body, culture/nature, reason/emotions, objectivity/subjectivity, rationality/irrationality, public/private.

The different characteristics, values and activities of the sexes have often been expressed through such dualisms. Men and the masculine are associated with the spirit, culture, reason, objectivity and rationality, and much of men's activity is traditionally linked to the public sphere. Women and the feminine are associated with the body, nature, emotions, subjectivity and irrationality, and typically female activities are linked to the private sphere. The male way of thinking is also normatively based and entails ethical choices. Certain qualities and values are usually to be preferred to others, or have at any rate more importance attached to them than others: the qualities, values and activities are ranked in a hierarchy. When they are linked to sex, a pattern is at the same time designed whereby one sex is subordinated to the other.[2]

There is nothing in itself wrong with dualisms and dichotomies. It is the meaning attached to them and the use to which they are put that must be questioned. Dual concepts are of course also included as analytical categories in women's research, for the obvious reason that there happen to be two and only two sexes. Some of the dichotomies mentioned above have indeed occupied a central position in research on the situation of women. They have formed meeting points in the description of how men have interpreted and treated women and womanliness, and of how women have been defined, not in relation to themselves but in relation to men. The concepts have moreover been given new meaning as a result of their being experienced and used in a dependent, non-separate, relational context within "circular" units: the spirit is body, culture is nature, thought is emotion etc. This is also emphasized by those engaged in women's research in discussions of different theoretical and methodological questions (Harding (ed.) 1987, Belenky et al. 1986, Smith 1987). I shall discuss this in greater detail below, partly through different appreciations of the nature of the birth process.

The Birth Process in a Matriarchal and a Patriarchal Perspective

In medical literature, the birth process is usually regarded as a linear process from beginning to end, divided into different evolutionary stages that succeed one another – from conception to breastfeeding. This linear way of understanding is not, as I have already indicated, directly in line with the more female "circular" and relational way of understanding. When a woman relates her experiences in connection with birth, her experiences usually appear as a wholeness, in which the different aspects of the experience become interwoven in other ways than the more step-like linear ones. Women's accounts may appear haphazard and give the impression of an inability to relate coherently, but the explanation is to be found in a type of experience structure which differs from what is, for instance, to be found in the gynaecology and obstetrics of medical science.

In Norway, Marianne Fastvold has for some years pointed out and criticized the way in which the birth process is split up in the practices of the public health service, and the participation of different professions in the different stages of the birth process. This fragmentation is also reflected in the legal provisions relating to the birth process (Fastvold 1990). Many feminist researchers have discussed the alienation which in many ways has taken place as a result of the medical profession having taken over the supervision of the birth process, and the subordination of midwives to medical practitioners and medical technology, and partly also to nurses (Oakley 1984, Ehrenreich 1973, Rich 1977, Hellum 1987).

The Finnish philosopher Camilla Cedercreutz has made an interesting contribution to the description of the alienation that has taken place. In her thesis on "Motherhood as a corporal experience and the specific knowledge it includes", she points out fundamental differences in matriarchal and patriarchal ways of understanding and practice (Cedercreutz 1989). It is worth relating the essence of her analysis of various birth-rites, with special emphasis on the practical and symbolic significance of the birth position.

Birth in an upright position was formerly common, and it is still the usual position in many cultures. Cedercreutz shows how this natural matriarchal position has given way to the patriarchal recumbent position, "a position which conflicts not only with inner knowledge but also with the law of gravity". On the symbolic level, the recumbent position involves the expression of a position of power. The person standing over has power. The recumbent position also entails that contact with earth and heaven are broken. Maternal godesses are often depicted with their feet on the earth and their arms raised to heaven – an expression of creative power and strength. The recumbent position is an expression of passivity. It is also associated with the image of a sick person, a person who needs medical aid (ibid., pp. 3 and 78).

Through the medical profession's quite comprehensive participation in and control of the birth process, the associations with sickness have become prominent generally. The legal provisions concerning the grant of maternity benefit during pregnancy, birth and post-natal care are to be found in chapter 3 of the National Insurance Act concerning *Cash benefit during illness and birth*. In 1952, it was decided that the first two years of training for midwives in Norway should follow the same program as the training of nurses.

The diagnostic routines and facilities offered by the public health control agencies during pregnancy and in the case of fertility problems have developed at an accelerating rate, with medical expertise and modern reproduction technology as driving forces. This development ever more strongly encourages thoughts about dangers, errors and malformations, and childlessness is discussed and treated in these contexts as an illness. The childless, the pregnant and the birth-giver become more and more patients and objects for medical surveillance, treatment and operation instead of subjects in a natural and healthy process (Koch 1987, Hellum 1990, Fastvold 1990, Aasen 1991).

Like Cedercreutz, one can wonder why Finnish – and Norwegian – women quietly accept the weakening effect that the recumbent position and other rites in the course of the birth process which point in the same direction entail: an established ranking of men and women, dichotomically based on power and subordination, activity and passivity, culture and nature, health and illness, even in situations that are typically womanly. But it is not *so* remarkable, since the organization of the birth process forms part of a far greater *cultural hegemony* based on such principles. The very essence of a cultural hegemony is that a particular group's special way of regarding and organizing the social realities is accepted as general and as a part of the natural order, also by those who are in fact subordinated to it. The practice becomes *so* inculcated and the values *so* self-evident that ordinarily no one gives them a thought. But the daily experiences among those who are subordinated are also stored as conscious possibilities for a socially reforming counter-culture.

It has been asserted that in order to change a culture, one must change the way people are born into the culture. Even though this is a somewhat simplified expression, it indicates the centrality of birth in the organization of society and the need for women's knowledge and policy based on birth law.

Elements of the Birth Process

How then can an analytical understanding of the birth process be reached if we are to avoid dividing it into the artificial, more or less limited, linear phases and stages, and instead try to capture the unity in the birth process? I think that Mary O'Brien's examination of what she calls the "moments" of the birth process should be pursued (O'Brien 1981, pp. 47 f).

By moments O'Brien means determining, active factors which operate in a *related* way, at both the biological and conceptual levels, involving the interplay of *non-isolated events in time*. The central moments are: menstruation, ovulation, copulation, alienation, conception, gestation, labour, birth, appropriation and nurture.

There are important differences in the nature of the moments. Only two of them are common to both men and women: *copulation* and *nurture*. Nurture is a manifold concept covering both support in kind (breastfeeding, other nourishment and physical care), financial support (work for money) and intellectual support (upbringing). Within the birth process, which ebbs away as breastfeeding, amongst other things, comes to an end, it is direct support in kind which constitutes the basis. The fact that this is largely provided by the woman has also brought about a prolonged division of labour between the sexes, based on the societal dividing line between support in kind and financial support, a dividing line where the financial supporter is regarded as the "main supporter" from the legal point of view.

Only two of the moments are purely male: alienation and appropriation. *Alienation* refers to the man's delivery of sperm to the woman, which at the same time entails for him a corporal alienation in relation to the further process. He withdraws, retreats, and leaves the rest to the woman and the fortuity of fate. Appropriation refers to the man's social annexation of the child after the birth – the institutionalization and legalization of paternity in the patriarchal family.

The other elements are purely female, and are mostly involuntary in the sense that they take place as a natural process in the woman's body. Thus they constitute her particular experience: *menstruation*, *ovulation*, *conception*, *gestation*, *labour* and *birth*. The last three require effort and the use of strength. In Scandinavian women's law, we have therefore in this context talked about women's *birth work*, as a necessary, but economically not sufficiently valued, equivalent to work in the market. Socio-economic women's research is in the process of providing us with some of the implements we have lacked for ensuring the security of birth work both nationally and globally (Waring 1988).

Two quite different worlds of experience are revealed in the relationships which the two sexes have to the birth process. The man's experience is episodic, marked by discontinuity in proximity and distance, and protected by social and political institutions laid down in legal rules concerning sexuality, paternity and the family. The woman's experience is the unity of maternity within herself, in continuity and interplay between sexuality, the foetus and the child.

Women's world of experience is also regulated through the legal rules which have arisen from male experiences. But as a result of the principle of *the dual-track legal system* laid down in current law, as mentioned above, another set of rules also applies: rules relating to the protection and control of women's birth process, based on how men have regarded women and their relationship to women. It is only during the last decades that women have themselves begun to make their mark on the contents of the rules by participating to a greater extent as subjects in the legislative processes. The establishment of birth law as a separate field of law is part of this participation.

III. Birth Law

What is Birth Law?

The *subject* of birth law comprises all the legal provisions that apply to the "moments" of the birth process from menstruation to nurture. "Nurture" introduces another area of women's law – support law (Ketscher 1990, pp. 31–44). Support provisions – both financial support and support in kind – within birth law are usually limited to those which apply to babyhood, i.e. the first year of the child's life.

The *purpose* of birth law is complex and conflicting. The basic purpose is to provide a proper foundation for creating, preserving and developing life. But the provisions also make arrangements for preventing and aborting life, through rules relating to contraception and termination of pregnancy.

In current law, the relevant systems and fragments of rules are to be found scattered over the most diverse fields of law: criminal law, family law, succession law, private law, constitutional law, social security law and labour law, to give examples of the most traditional areas of jurisprudence in this connection, and the areas in which birth-law provisions were first introduced. If we proceed to a more modern systemization of jurisprudence, areas such as national insurance law, women's law, children's law, public health law and patient law are also included.

Given the strongly *fragmented and interdisciplinary nature* of the legal provisions within birth law, the need to collect them is immediately evident. There is a need to describe and evaluate the sets and fragments of rules, as far as possible collectively, within the entirety that the birth process constitutes in real life. Since the entirety in the birth process is the property of women, development of birth law as a separate field of law entails an assertion of the female norm in the law.

It is therefore natural that birth law as a separate legal field has arisen within women's law, as a distinct area of women's law. It was Marianne Fastvold in her undergraduate thesis *Fødselsrett og likhet – et kvinneperspektiv* (Birth Law and Equality – a Female Perspective) from 1977 who first used the expression birth law and began to collect some of the fragments of rules pertaining to this field (Fastvold 1977). It was also Fastvold who produced the first collective account of this field of law (Fastvold 1990).[3]

Since women are interwoven with the children they create and the men with whom they have a sexual relationship and possibly have children, the female perspective crosses the interests of both children and men as individuals and groups of persons with coinciding and conflicting interests. In addition to the individuals of which they are comprised, also the mother-child entity and the family constitute legal categories within many legal fields of community life.

The application of the female perspective is thus a person-directed methodological tactic based upon recognition of the *significance of sex* as a fundamental factor in the organization of society.

The Law as a Tradition

The law is a norm system whose authoritative effect on the citizens reflects the interdependence of society at any given time. The content of the norms is decided by the prevailing ideological trends and power relationships, but is by nature thoroughly conservative, partly because it takes time to set down the attitudes and customs of the different civic groups and because of the power struggle that lies behind the formal legislative compromises. But even before new legislation is implemented, the new trends will often influence the application of the law through statutory interpretation in individual cases, and they also influence general legal awareness.

Development of birth law as a separate field will thus serve to raise the general consciousness of the significance of this sphere of life, to influence the art of judicial interpretation, and to create a basis of knowledge for possible legislative amendments.

Current law is always the product of a long tradition. This tradition carries great weight, and the past always becomes a central part of the present and future in the legal system. Changes made through the law will thus entail a silent process, except in the case of a political coup and reform of the system. But even in the latter case this may be so, at any rate in a field such as birth law, which is so directly linked to existential human life and the everyday life, customs and rites of the citizens.

The past has thus created a patriarchal legal system in this sphere of life, based on the male elements in the birth process. In the course of time the matriarchal elements have forced their way in and resulted in a more equal status for women, with increased self-determination and control over the female elements in the birth process. In the last two decades we have seen the prevailing system and new elements in exciting interaction and movement towards the future. In the 1990s this movement will be subject to strong interference by technology and medical interests (see section IV). Among other possibilities for radical change, modern reproduction technology has for the first time in history made it possible to isolate a series of the "moments" of the birth process outside the woman's body – revolutionary events in the history of birth. The interaction between culture and nature in the work of creation is thus subject to a special challenge in our time, in relation to both maternity and paternity.

Paternity is based on the four male moments of the birth process: sexuality and *copulation*, the (temporary) *alienation* of the sperm to the chances of fate and the woman's care, the social *appropriation* of the child through the constitution of legal paternity, and also *nurture* in that the man is considered the family's main supporter from a legal point of view.

Let me take these elements as a starting point in order to describe some main features of the legal development, through the man's relationship to the woman, the child and the family. Such an approach will bring us first to *matrimonial law and criminal law*, the legal fields which have primarily regulated sexual intercourse and cohabitation between spouses; next to *family law and social welfare law*, which primarily regulate appropriation and support, i.e. the social and economic aspects of paternity and the distribution of authority and work relating to parental responsibility. Since the matriarchal elements have forced their way in, both matrimonial law and large areas of the criminal law have lost their significance in the sphere of the birth process, whereas others, such as public health law, labour law, children's law etc. have been introduced. Family law and social welfare law still occupy a central position.

Matrimonial Law and Criminal Law

In earlier times, sexual intercourse was strictly regulated by matrimonial law and criminal law. Legislation following the Reformation as published in the *Norwegian Laws of King Christian the Fifth* of 1687 provided that civil status should determine what was lawful and unlawful voluntary sexuality (including concubinage, prostitution and fornication). Unlawful sexuality outside marriage was regarded to be more serious from the criminal law point of view if one or both parties were married. Women were the most severely judged. The *Criminal Code* of 1842 both reduced and partly abolished the criminality of voluntary sexual intercourse, but the principles remained. Sexual liberation continued with the enactment of the *Penal Code* of 1902 which is now in force, and the amendments made thereto during the twentieth century, both formally and through the art of judicial interpretation.

Through marriage, the man acquired free access to *his* woman, control of other men's access to her and control of his wife's immorality. As the master of the marriage, he had legal authority over the couple's financial and social decisions, as well as over their sexual practice. He thus had control over the frequency of sexual intercourse and the depositing of sperm.

Rape in marriage was a contradiction in terms until far into the twentieth century. Criminal law experts and family law specialists asserted that rape in marriage was legally impossible and that sexual intercourse was a matrimonial obligation. Entering into marriage was thus from a legal point of view considered to be a prior consent to sexual intercourse.

These arguments have in a modified – and more doubtful – form been put forward even in post-war legal text-books. It was not until the 1970s that the Norwegian Supreme Court declared that rape in marriage must basically be regarded on a par with rape outside marriage (Rt. 1971, p. 873 and Rt. 1974, p. 1121). Thus we have here an example of a change in the law through the art of judicial interpretation, which is influenced by the altered position of women in society.

As regards sexual assaults outside marriage, the Norwegian Law of 1687 divided women into categories that were more or less worthy of protection: the virtuous maiden, the good wife and the immoral woman. Today it is no longer the man's "property" which is accorded the protection of the criminal law, but the citizens' sexual freedom, including the right of all women to self-determined sexuality. Nevertheless a good many traces of the old tradition are to be found in the sentencing practice of the courts. The traditional way of thinking plays a part in both modern preparatory works before statute, and in the judges' evaluation of the victim's "guilt" in rape cases, for instance, on the basis of what risk situation she put herself in (Agerup 1990, Dahl 1990b, Ysen 1989).

Even today, marriage has a certain significance for defining unpunishable sexuality; a penalty is not imposed and a conviction is deprived of its effect if the offender subsequently marries his victim (the Penal Code, s.214). This no longer applies to the most serious sexual crimes such as rape. In former times even kidnapping a bride could be shielded by subsequent marriage.

The patriarchal birth law also contains criminal provisions which control the purely female elements in the process: induced abortion, surreptitious childbirth, infanticide and farming out children, guidance in or encouraging the use of contraceptives. Previously, such violations of the law were often prosecuted, and sometimes severely punished, e.g. with the death penalty for infanticide (Gotaas 1980). Punishment for induced abortion was abolished for women in 1975, while at the same time the indications in favour of abortion were widely extended through the passing of the *Termination of Pregnancy Act* of 13 June 1975. In 1978, women's demand for self-determined abortion was granted, as long as the abortion can be performed before the expiry of the twelfth week of pregnancy (the Abortion Act, s.2(2)).

As regards infanticide and the farming out of children etc., there are now several provisions which provide for these criminal acts to be treated *more leniently* if they are committed by the mother within 24 hours of the birth. If a woman kills her child, or gets rid of it, or abandons it in a helpless state, the penalties applicable are lower than is otherwise the case (Penal Code, ss.234 and 244), and there is a special penal provision which applies to a man who avoids rendering assistance to a woman in need in connection with her pregnancy and delivery where he has made her pregnant (Penal Code, s.240).

As we see, the development in the criminal law has recognized women's right to equal status in sexual life, i.e. *self-determined sexuality*, and the regulation of sexuality has been entirely liberated from the bonds of marriage: women's self-determination within marriage has been legally established, and women's sexuality outside marriage has been decriminalized. This explains the dramatic fall over time in the number of women's sexual offences (Høigård 1983).

However, current criminal law does to a great degree concern women as *victims* of sexual assaults. Chapter 19 of the Penal Code relating to Sexual Crimes penalizes assaults on women's sexual freedom (rape and acts akin to rape), as well as the sexual exploitation of one's own children, other persons' children, young people (incest, sexual assaults on minors) and other particularly exposed groups (including the disabled and the mentally ill). On closer inspection it appears that it is almost exclusively men who are the offenders, while women (both adults and minors) and boys constitute the victims (Ysen 1989, Agerup 1990, Wesenberg 1990).

Likewise, women have gained the right to *self-determined pregnancy* through the abortion legislation of the 1970s. It is, however, the liberation and technological development of contraception that has created the revolutionary degree of control that enables the commencement of pregnancy to be voluntary. Mary O'Brien calls this a "world historical event" in the Hegelian sense, that women themselves can decide whether, when and how many times they will give birth. When this is combined with women's access to education, she believes that our time is a completely new age, which might be called "The Age of Contraception" on a par with "The Age of Industrialism" (O'Brien 1981, pp. 21f). Since the prohibition against advertising has ceased to apply, there is now no special legislation relating to contraception, apart from the Abortion Act, s.14(a) which gives an explicit right to guidance as to forms of contraception following an abortion. Moreover, guidance and help with contraception must be considered on a par with other public health services pursuant to the *Act relating to Municipal Health Services* of 1982 and the obligation of the various professions to give information and assistance pursuant to the *Medical Practitioners Act* of 1980 and the *Midwives Act* of 1985. On the other hand, there is a statutory right to sterilization for those over 25 years of age provided they are not mentally ill or mentally retarded, cf. the *Sterilization Act* of 1977. This Act also contains provisions concerning compulsory sterilization and castration, which have been applied in social law and criminal law. The Sterilization Act was extended by the occupying Nazi forces during the second world war through *Act No. 1 for the Protection of the National Lineage*, partly on the German model, as part of the Nazi policy of population quality control. In the preparatory works to the Act, it was contended that in the absence of technological possibilities for *positive* quality control, one had to content oneself with the *negative* form that sterilization entails. Today, medical science has also developed possibilities for positive control in the form of gene control and foetus diagnostics, combined with facilities for abortion and operation on the foetus. The short leap between the two situations is thought-provoking and requires an ethical examination of our views on human dignity (Aasen 1990a, Nordborg 1987).

Through women's access to contraception and abortion, the man has lost much of his previous ability to control whether and when he will transfer his sperm to the woman and the fortuity of fate. Nor is it any longer fate which dictates the result. The woman can bar the way to fertilization, abolish its effects, or admit the man's sperm, independently of his expectations and his knowledge. From a legal point of view, it is the public health legislation which sets the practical limits for the operation of these vital processes.

Family Law and Social Law

So what about the patriarchal elements – appropriation and support (nurture)? What about paternity's legal relation to the child and to the mother-child entity?

The legal principle upon which paternity's social and economic effects within the framework of the family were based was the "pater est" rule. "Pater est quem nuptiae demonstrant" – the marriage shows who the father is. This maxim has throughout the ages afforded legal protection to both the father, children and mother – and hence to the family as an institution. The father of the family did not need to question whether it was *his* child unless he himself wished to contest paternity. From the moment of conception, the foetus acquired social and economic rights which were further extended at the child's birth: the right of succession and allodial rights, citizenship, a name and a right to support from the father of the family. The mother also acquired a further right of support for herself and her child, through statutory provisions relating to the obligations of maintenance and care.

The patriarchal family had the man as its head. He was the family representative externally in society, and society's representative internally in the family. Legal rules were constructed around this comprehensive role of authority and supporter. He had the right to administer the family's property and income, and authority over everyday decisions; he was regarded as the supporter, and subsequently – when women entered more into men's life – as the main supporter. The husband's and father's role as supporter is linked to his provision of financial support through labour law, tax law and national insurance law. Within the family he also had a role in upbringing, through discipline, chastisement and love. If these internal obligations were overstepped or neglected, he could be found to be in breach of the provisions of the Penal Code relating to Crimes concerning Family Relations. He could also lose his child to the state through provisions in the poor law or the Child Welfare Act.

The general trend has been towards increased "publicizing of the family" (Hernes 1982b). From a legal point of view, social law occupies a central position in this trend. The first major encroachment made by social law upon the autocracy of paternity were the *Castbergian Children's Acts* of 1915, popularly so called after Norway's first Minister of Social Affairs, Johan Castberg, a member of Gunnar Knudsen's liberal government. As a result of the Children's Acts of 1915, children born out of wedlock acquired some of the rights of legitimate children, including a limited right of succession and a right to support. In the industrialized world, the Norwegian man was the first to be made economically liable for the sperm he deposited in any woman and to be compelled to partly accept the child.

The Children's Acts of 1915 were in many ways the first step towards recognizing the *mother-child family*; children born out of wedlock and the mothers of these children were now no longer left to the uncertain response of mere charity or driven out into the gutter. In recent times this form of family has become ever more widespread and gained stronger legal protection. Recognition of the mother-child family, together with the abolition of marriage as the guardian of sexuality, has entailed that unmarried cohabitation, both with and without children, has also become quite widespread during the 1970s and 1980s. Legal questions arising in relation to couples who live together unmarried, with or without children, have become so frequent that *unmarried cohabitation* has today developed into a new and separate area of law. The previous uncertain use of such concepts as "common-law marriage", "cohabitation agreement" etc. are now well rooted in unmarried cohabitation as an alternative legal relationship to marriage, and Kirsti Strøm Bull has now given a collective account of this legal relationship (Bull 1990). With the rift that unmarried cohabitation has made in matrimonial law, and the rift that the mother-child family has made in family law, one can join Kirsten Ketscher in asking whether family law is now in a process of dissolution (Ketscher 1989).

The mother-child family has a relatively strong position in Norwegian society today, even though we must admit that many of these families are among the poorest in the welfare state. Equal status between children born in and out of wedlock is almost complete after the *Children Act* of 1981. A controversial question during the preparation of the Act was whether the "pater est" rule should be abolished in marriage, but it was retained in the interests of family peace – a point of view I fully share.

It is possible to survive on the benefits granted under the *Child Allowance Act* of 1946 and chapters 10 and 12 relating to single supporters in the *National Insurance Act* of 1966. Single supporters (unmarried, separated, divorced and widowed persons) receive child allowance for one child extra, and the national insurance system ensures an extra maternity grant and a minimum standard of maintenance for mother and child through their right to transitional benefit, educational benefit and child care benefit. The benefits can generally be maintained until the youngest child reaches 10 years of age if the mother does not have or is not expected to obtain paid work. But most mother-child families survive on the mother's paid work and maintenance payments from the father, regulated by the Children's Act and the *Act relating to Maintenance in Advance* of 1989.

Also within the family, paternity and the man's marriage has lost much of its dominance. The man's and the woman's authority are formally equal, as is also his and her right to administer property and income. In reality, inequality still exists because of his far greater possibilities of acquiring capital and income. In the new allodial rights legislation, however, the *Act relating to Allodial Matters* of 1974 has made a substantial encroachment upon men's preferential right to land, by making the allodial and primogeniture rights of daughters equal to those of sons. Maternity has lost a certain precedence through the abolition of the prior right the mother previously had to the custody of the child after divorce. But maternity has also gained a right; quite surprisingly Norwegian name law has formally become matriarchal. By the *Personal Names Act* of 1964, women became fully entitled to retain their maiden name upon marriage. Their identity too is thereby liberated from marriage. A statutory amendment of 1979 then provided that the children of a marriage shall take the mother's name unless the parents give notice to the contrary (the Names Act, s.2). It is many years since the right of the head of the family to chastise his children, wife and servants was abolished. In the last decade it is rather the criminal violence of dominance which has been brought to light and dealt with.

It is with regard to the last element of the birth process, *support*, that there is a great gap between formal and real equality, and this applies to both care support and financial support. The man's and the woman's support of each other, their children and themselves had already been put on an equal footing in family law by the *Act relating to the Property Relationship between the Spouses* of 1927. Since "financial subsidies" were equated with "work in the home" in the mutual obligation to maintain each other and the children, support in kind was accorded the same legal status as financial support. This equality in private law has not, however, been followed up in public law. In labour law, national insurance law and tax law, for instance, it is a male norm that prevails, cf. above under section I.

The relationship between *special protective provisions* for women in industrial life on the one hand and women's interests on the other has throughout its history been a matter of controversy, as regards both the right to special consideration in the working environment, maternity and welfare leave, and prohibition against night work.

Women's groups pursuing equal status have been concerned that such special protective provisions would weaken women's competitiveness on the paid-work market, whereas others have been most concerned with reasonable working conditions during the birth process. It is true to say that women's childbearing role has proved to be a competitive handicap on the labour market. It has also been the case that male trade unions have tried to support special protective provisions for women in order to weaken their competitive ability, as the printers did at the beginning of this century. By supporting a prohibition against night work for women, they hoped to secure themselves against the low wages paid to women, by excluding women during some of the hours when there was a great demand for work (Hagemann 1973, Ertesvåg 1975). Women workers in other countries experienced much the same.

It has also been the case that attempts have been made to exclude women of childbearing age from specific workplaces, with the justification that they should not work under environmental conditions that would expose them to any risk of damage to the foetus.

During the preparatory works to the Working Environment Act and the amendments thereto, such views were put forward but subsequently rejected. *Foetus protection* has, however, recently appeared more and more often on the agenda, especially in the USA. After losing in the lower court, an American entrepreneur recently succeeded in the appellate court in his claim to exclude women of child-bearing age from most of the jobs in his battery-producing enterprises, on the grounds of "the employer's foetus protection policy" (International Union vs Johnson Controls 886 F. 2 d 871 (7th Cir. 1989)). In Norway, too, there are protective provisions against foetus damage, but primarily in the form of an individual right to relocation for pregnant women, and various forms of protection in a health-risk working environment.

The protective provisions in current law are to be found in the *Working Environment Act* of 1977. This Act has a separate chapter concerning the right to maternity leave during pregnancy and birth etc. There are also provisions relating to the right to a safe place of work, relocation, reduced working hours and safeguards against dismissal during pregnancy and maternity leave. The maternity leave provisions secure the right to return to work after the end of maternity leave.

It is clear that such protective provisions have a particular effect on women's ability to compete in the market. One of the objects of the *Act relating to Equal Status between the Sexes* of 1978 is therefore to put the competitive ability of the sexes on an equal footing by prohibiting sex discrimination in the case of appointment, pay and promotion. These provisions have not, however, proved to be particularly effective in practice (Halvorsen 1985a and b).

The provisions of the Working Environment Act are supplemented by the *National Insurance Act* of 1966, which confers a right to a grant in the form of pay or a cash benefit following a birth. In these provisions, the male norm of the wage-earner state is clearly revealed. The entitlement is to a grant in the form of full pay during the woman's pregnancy leave and mother's care leave. Fathers are not entitled to paid leave in connection with their children's births. The provisions for unpaid care-leave are weak and are rarely used by fathers. Women who are not on the labour market are fobbed off with a small single grant intended to compensate them for expenses connected with their birth work.

Today, nearly all births take place in maternity institutions or on the way to them (because of the great geographical distances involved, a large number of births in Norway occur during transportation), and they are thus subject to *hospital and medical practice legislation*, with ordinary patient rights for the woman giving birth. In addition, there are special provisions concerning parental responsibility. *The Children Act* of 1981 provides in s.2 that the mother is entitled to have the father of the child – or another person close to her – present at the birth. The joint parental responsibility with the obligation and right to exercise care of the child pursuant to s.30 of the Children Act arises at the moment the child is born. In this field, a lot could be done to improve the right to information, participation and legal safeguards, both where the birth is normal and when something goes wrong (Fastvold 1985a, Bull 1985a).

Female and Male Norm

My exposition has shown how birth law has been organized within a patriarchal legal system based on the male elements in the birth process. Over time, this system has been imbued with a number of matriarchal elements, which collectively can be said to be so fundamental that in several respects it would be appropriate to speak of the dissolution of the patriarchal tradition.

In the sphere of sexuality, women have formally been put on an equal with men, and, as a starting point, they themselves decide whether they will get involved and whether they will have sexual intercourse. But sexual freedom also has another aspect in that many men now have stronger expectations that all women are to be seen as a possible sexual object. In real life, a good many women are exposed to sexual assaults, and in everyday life there is also sexual harassment in the workplace, in leisure hours and via the pornography industry, as a source of pressure on women's integrity and the quality of their lives.

In the family sphere, women have also gained formal equality internally. But in this instance too, the realities of life are harsher than the legal ones, as regards both equal division of work, sexual freedom and other bodily integrity, and this reality no doubt is part of the explanation for the spreading of the mother-child family and unmarried cohabitation – the new legal institutions which now compete with the traditional family institution. These new forms of cohabitation, however, also present challenges: laborious efforts and poverty in the first case, and not infrequently little legal security in the second.

At last, women have gained a greater degree of self-determination and control over several of the female elements of the birth process. This is particularly the case with fertilization, through access to contraception and the right to abortion. With regard to pregnancy and care, however, much remains to be done. Birth and care work operate in an economic and legal grey area, which, in conjunction with the labour market policy, leads to an over-consumption of women's labour and health, and an unfair distribution of the money flow in society. Women's, children's and family life are thus exposed to strains that, in my opinion, are neither appropriate nor worthy of our type of welfare state.

Altogether women have gained a greater degree of self-determination and control over the female elements of the birth process, while the legal institutions which were constructed around the male elements of the birth process have been weakened. The female norm has thus gained ground in the field of birth law, while a reduction of the male norm has occurred, especially through the establishment of sexual freedom as an individual principle, and through dissolutionary trends in family law.

This does not of itself mean that the male norm has been weakened in relation to women's life and living conditions as a whole. My exposition has indeed shown how the male norm has been strengthened in other areas, primarily through assertion of the primary of the labour market and the legal institutions of paid work.

This last trend also traverses birth law. Just as the market threatens the family's various cohabitational forms, the market in certain respects threatens the self-determination and control acquired by women over several of the female elements of the birth process. What I have in mind is birth technology and the development in public health law.

IV. Reproduction Technology. Maternity and Paternity

So far, I have avoided the term "reproduction", preferring the terms birth and care, birth process and birth policy. Reproduction calls to mind something secondary, something less important than the original/main issue. Economic and Marxist thinking have accorded primacy to production. In such contexts, the tasks of reproduction have often been analysed in view of the market's need for maintaining and promoting an adequate workforce, instead of being dealt with as a fundamental sphere of life in its own right. Materially, and therefore conceptually, birth technology occupies a special position, since it is developed and applied within the market, and because market and professional interests are today powerful driving forces in this field.

In a wide sense, reproduction technology may be defined as all types of birth technology, but I will here apply a narrow definition: technology applied in connection with fertilization and foetus development. The types of technology particularly involved are *artificial insemination, test-tube fertilization, pre-natal diagnosis and foetus medicine.*

Reproduction technology can make dramatic incursions into the mother-child entity. In the first place, it makes it possible to separate several of the elements of the birth process from the woman's body: ovulation, copulation, alienation, conception and the commencement of pregnancy. Secondly, it offers opportunities to intervene in the woman's body during pregnancy, in order to diagnose and, if necessary, treat the foetus.

I agree with Ingse Stabel that the day it became possible to fertilize a human ovum outside the womb and thereafter to implant it again in the woman's body, an irreversible step was taken in the history of birth technology and the human race. By breaking the unity between womb and ovum, one of the most fundamental institutions in human family and social life was broken (Stabel 1988).

This must, of course, have consequences for fundamental legal views and concepts linked to legal rights and morality, control and protection, generational responsibility and ecological considerations (Tranøy 1989, Frost 1989, Hellum et al. 1990). In our context, the effect of the technology on legal views concerning maternity and paternity is of central importance.

Until now, paternity has been a legal construction, since the father-child connection has never been a biologically certain and given fact. Paternity is therefore constituted as described through various legal institutions, and it can also be renounced through legal rules. Maternity cannot be renounced except by adoption, nor does it need any legal construction in order to be established. The mother-child entity is a given and incontestable fact, both genetically and biologically, and therefore also legally (Stabel 1988).

Test-tube technology now forces us to distinguish between three possible types of legal maternity: *the genetic mother*, from whom the ovum is derived; *the biological mother*, who carries out the pregnancy and birth; *the social mother*, who has parental responsibility for the child. Until now, these three have all been one and the same, but from now on, mothers can operate in triplicate or in different combinations. When we supplement the natural method or the test-tube method with artificial insemination, with fresh or deep-frozen sperm, from a known or unknown donor, paternity is also subjected to new legal forms and combinations. Finally, parenthood as a whole and the legal provisions relating to parental responsibility acquire a new content. We are faced with "a reproductive chaos" (Hellum 1987).

According to the *Artificial Procreation Act* of 1987, current law in Norway is quite restrictive, even compared to the other Scandinavian countries, as regards both artificial insemination and test-tube fertilization.

By artificial insemination is meant the introduction of sperm into a woman's vagina or cervix otherwise than through sexual intercourse. It is a matter of low-level technology which has been practised in hospitals in Norway for years on the basis of an ethic of medical selection and a queue system for the facilities. Today, this insemination service can only be provided by authorized institutions, and only such institutions may freeze and otherwise store sperm. There is no legal right to this service and it is still the case that it is a doctor who assesses and decides whether such aid shall be given, and who selects a suitable sperm donor, who remains unknown to the parties. But legal constraints have been imposed on the doctors: in Norway, artificial insemination shall only be given within marriage, and the husband must be infertile or the carrier of a serious hereditary disease (the Artificial Procreation Act, ss.2 to 10).

Test-tube fertilization is fertilization of an ovum outside the woman's body. This involves expensive high-level technology, which is in current Norwegian law subject to severe restrictions: the treatment is only available to married couples, only when the woman is sterile, e.g. because of a fault in the fallopian tubes, and only with the couple's own ova and sperm cells. Fertilized ova may only be returned to the woman from whom they are derived, they can only be stored for up to 12 months, and it is prohibited to carry out research on fertilized ova. The freezing of fertilized ova is prohibited (the Artificial Procreation Act, ss.1 to 5, 11, 12).

The opposite to Norway is the USA, where there is no legislation concerning artificial procreation, and where the field is strongly commercialized. Childless couples who can afford to pay constitute a large market. Private sperm banks have been established; advertisements are placed for "surrogate mothers", or "contract mothers", which is perhaps a better description. Contracts are entered into for the implanting of the woman's own ova fertilized with the husband's or another man's sperm, or of ova donated by another woman; or the woman herself donates ova which are fertilized and implanted in another woman, who is hired to bear the child. Here, the many possible combinations of maternity and paternity are to be found in practice, and they have given rise to a series of law suits concerning what one can bind oneself to do and whether one can change one's mind.

The most notorious case so far – the "Baby M" case – which went to the Court of Appeal in the State of New Jersey, has created a certain degree of legal clarity, but also some uncertainty concerning motherhood by contract (Matter of Baby M, 109 N.J. 396, 537 A. 2d 1227 (1988), Olsen 1988). A woman had entered into a contract to bear a man's child and then to surrender the child to him and his wife in return for a payment of 10000 dollars. She gave birth to the child, but then wished to keep it and therefore to rescind the contract. The lower court found that she was bound by the contract, ordered her to surrender the child to the father, and allowed his wife to adopt it. The Court of Appeal, however, declared that the contract in the case implied that the mother relinquished her parental right in return for a money payment, which the court regarded as a sort of "child sale", contrary to morality and the laws of New Jersey. The payment to the surrogate mother was therefore also unlawful and perhaps criminal. The Court of Appeal annulled the social mother's adoption of the child, since it was the biological mother who had the parental rights. But the court allowed the biological father to retain custody, considering that this was in the best interests of the child. The biological mother thus lost both the child and the money. However, the judgment in the Baby M case should help to counteract future contracts of this type. As long as it is unlawful to receive payment, agreements to function as the biological mother for another man/woman will presumably rarely be of practical interest. But there are nevertheless many types of agreements that are unaffected by this judgment, and so far it applies only in the State of New Jersey.

Foetus Diagnostics and Foetus Medicine

By foetus diagnostics, or pre-natal diagnostics, are meant medical services offered to pregnant women – to all of them or to specific risk groups – which comprise various types of medical examinations of the foetus, in particular ultrasonic examinations, amniotic fluid tests and placenta tests. The diagnostic methods can ascertain the exact date when pregnancy began, and the development and state of health of the foetus can partly be followed. Certain chromosome faults, inherited diseases and malformations can be discovered, and the technological development is so rapid that it must be expected that in the near future it will be possible to detect a great number of risks and malformations in the foetus.

Such examinations have a dual purpose, both of which can have far-reaching consequences for women and for the mother-child entity. Foster diagnostics aim predominantly at creating the best possible conditions for the development of the foetus. But foster diagnostics are also concerned with examinations whose purpose is to register diseases, risks and malformations which may possibly warrant abortion (Aasen 1990b and 1991).

Research in connection with foetus diagnostics and artificial procreation, especially test-tube fertilization, has constantly increased the visibility of the foetus. The foetus can be seen in all its stages in films and illustrations; we know more and more about its appearance, state of health, what affects it, its hereditary qualities, degree of development and potentiality. It stands out for us, separately from the mother.

Again, we are faced with changes in fundamental legal views. Traditionally, the foetus has been entirely dependent on the physical protection afforded it by the mother's body, and its legal position has been in accordance with this. It has not been accorded independent legal status except in quite special contexts (for instance, in the law of succession). Reproduction technology has strengthened our knowledge of, and thereby our recognition of, *the foetus as a possible legal entity* in its own right (Stabel 1988, Hellum 1987). This has provided grounds for new discussions concerning when life really begins, and concerning the foetus as a patient, and foetus protection generally (Johnsen 1990).

Until now, it has been almost indisputable that the woman must be presumed to be the closest to make the best decisions on behalf of the whole mother-child entity as regards questions connected with health and life-style, including the fundamental question as to whether a pregnancy should be terminated. Technology has produced new interest groups and reactivated old ones who wish to speak on behalf of the foetus. When the foetus becomes a patient, medical research, doctors, public health and social welfare personnel will all have a word to say. In the USA, a court judgment has authorized compulsory surgical intervention in the mother's body in order to treat the foetus (Johnsen 1990), and through the new concept of "foetal abuse", maltreatment of the foetus, there are grounds for intervening in the mother's living conditions and life-style, forcibly if necessary, if improvements in them are not effected according to the recommendations made by public health and social welfare personnel.

As regards the second purpose of foetus diagnostics – the prevention of illness and suffering by revealing damage to the foetus and risks of disease – women are confronted with expectations and choices of a very difficult nature. The alternative of abortion lies implicit in the facilities offered by foster diagnostics. The abortion debate has now been given a new substance, highlighting the matter of "selective abortions" – the question of abortion when there is something wrong with the foetus. Once again we are faced with fundamental views – this time the view of human dignity (Aasen 1990b).

Foetus diagnostics are also referred to in official reports as preventive public health work and linked to abortion (Aasen 1991), but there are no formal norms in Norwegian society which define those forms of life which are worth living. In principle, Norwegian society has no definition of undesirable hereditary qualities. Pragmatic social thinking on eugenic grounds is not a legitimate argument for foetus diagnostics.

The public health service and public policy have made the choice private, but how free is the choice? The woman is left with a heavy responsibility for subjecting life to suffering and disease. Studies show that women find it difficult not to accept the facilities they are offered for foetus diagnostics. If the results are negative, it is also difficult to refrain from abortion (Aasen 1991).

Reproduction technology presents many challenges. One of them is to balance the significance of this technology in an appropriate manner from the point of view of birth law. On the one hand, it is clear that the application of the technology is marginal when viewed in relation to the normal course of pregnancy and birth. Facilities for test-tube fertilization, for instance, are few and concern only a minority of those giving birth. The problems presented in birth law will continue to be those that are raised through the normal course of conception, pregnancy, birth and care work. On the other hand, reproduction technology raises questions which, even though they are peripheral, nevertheless concern the whole field, in as far as the technology draws the line between the natural and the humanly manipulated course. From a legal point of view, such dividing lines will aways be of interest, because the concepts that are used to deal with the main subject-matter are constituted by a demarcation of the outer limits.

Reproduction technology is developed with a market institution, where one of the groups participating in the market is childless couples or individuals, and another is mothers or parents anxious about having malformed children and who are encouraged by doctors to seek the facilities offered. The party offering the facilities in the market is made up of powerful forces such as bioindustry, biotechnology, medicine, the public health service – factors that decide not only what shall be offered but also define – and constantly extend – the limits for what can be requested.

How this market, with its still marginal extent in relation to normal birth, will influence the social view of the substance of birth, we do not know. But we should be well advised to expect that some form of influence will occur, and that the norms for womanliness and manliness and the relationship between them will be subjected to pressure.

With the pressure exerted by the labour market's male equal-status claims on the one hand, and a technology market in full development on the other, the limits for the future of the female norm may altogether be restricted. In this situation it is, in my opinion, even more important now than it was previously to strengthen birth law as a nucleus for the development of women's legal position, and thereby of the quality of human life generally.

Notes

* This article was first published in *Nye kvinner, nye menn*, ed. by Runa Haukaa, Oslo, 1991.

1 Concerning "the dual-track legal system" in national insurance law and tax law respectively see Sverdrup 1984 and 1985. Various welfare rights are studied in the areas of women's law known as money law (Dahl 1982), housewives law (Fastvold & Hellum 1985, Bull 1985b), paid-work law (Nielsen 1978, Halvorsen 1985a and b, Dahl 1985b, Petersen 1987 and 1990) and support law (Ketscher 1990).

2 The following accounts of the dichotomies, their use and significance, are instructive: Jaggar 1983, Moller-Okin 1979, Keller 1985, Harding 1986, Pateman & Gross (eds.) 1986. See also Haavind (1989) with a "dichotomic" attack by Elster (1990).

3 Besides the works referred to in this article, further bibliographical guidance is given in annotated bibliographies by Johnsen (1989) and Pedersen (1989).

2

Legal Safeguards During Birth*

MARIANNE FASTVOLD

Introduction

In birth law the main person is the woman who gives birth, here called the birth-worker. She is the one who is totally involved, both physically and psychologically, through her biological work during pregnancy and labour. It is obvious that she should play a central part in the development of society's birth policy. This has not happened: on the contrary, the birth-worker's responsibility and right to participate in decisions has been limited by legislation and practice.

The legislation relating to the termination of pregnancy has for a long time tended to limit the criteria for granting and preventing legal terminations of pregnancy as much as possible, by rendering women powerless to deal with this issue. Birth law is otherwise characterized by a lack of positive rights: to advice, assistance and guidance from health personnel. Besides the economic aspects, which will not be discussed here, birth work includes the physical, psychological and social aspects of which the pregnant parturient woman or her closest relatives need help in comprehending. If she is unable to comprehend these aspects, her participation in decisions will in practice be greatly reduced. It is some of these latter aspects of birth law that I want to discuss in greater detail below: the right to decide for oneself in the instance in which the health personnel's services are most necessary, i.e. during the birth. Today nearly all births take place in birth institutions or on the way to them.[1]

There is, however, a growing interest in home births, and these will be treated as a part of the whole picture.

Birth in an Institution

"Birth institutions" is a common term for all institutions that have the facilities and equipment for carrying out births; from small local maternity homes to large central hospitals with maternity wards. In practice the experience of birth differs greatly according to where one gives birth. The small maternity homes often have an intimate atmosphere that provides good personal contact with the staff and a feeling of security. Their weakness is that they often do not have the equipment and staff to cope with critical births, so that these must be referred to central hospitals, with the risks that entails. The large hospitals have the equipment and knowledge, but big wards and changing personnel create a more impersonal atmosphere. From a legal point of view, the rules are the same regardless of what type of institution one gives birth in.

The Birth-worker's Rights

The right to birth help was previously expressly laid down in the Midwives Act s.4. A midwife was obliged to give immediate help to women in "labour". Previously, doctors also had the same obligation, specifically laid down in the former Medical Practitioners Act s.7. The Midwives Act of 1898 has now been repealed, but a new Act is on its way. The public health services outside hospitals are dealt with in the Medical Practitioners Act s.7, which states: "A doctor is obliged, to give such help as he is able to give when he, according to the information available, must presume that medical aid is urgently needed. The obligation must presume that medical aid is urgently needed. The obligation lapses if the doctor has a valid excuse for absence, or knows that help will be given in time by another doctor."

Birth help is not specifically mentioned any more, but is generally included according to the preparatory works (Ot. prp. no. 1 (1979–80):235f.). The exception provisions in the Midwives Act were narrower than those in the Medical Practitioners Act. The midwife is only excused if she "is prevented because she is giving birth help to somebody else or if she is ill" (s.4(1)). The Midwives Act of 1898 only applied to district midwives.

Moreover, it is laid down in s.6 of the Hospital Act that hospitals and maternity homes are obliged to "receive a patient without delay when it is urgently necessary", as it will be when labour has started. The exception provision is narrow (the Hospital Act s.6(2)); the hospital is only excused if it has ascertained that help can be given by another institution closer to hand. Any contravention of the obligation is subject to a penalty (the Medical Practitioners Act, ss.52 and 53, the Hospital Act, s.6(4)).

Generally, it must be said that the right to help in childbirth is well established by statute. In practice there will, of course, be limitations on the extent to which a law can actually be applied. The distance to the hospital is, for instance, completely decisive. The hospital/maternity home policy – with the abolition of small maternity units under discussion is of central significance in this respect (St. meld. no. 9 (1974–75) Hospitals Development in a Regionalized Public Health Service: 66, 58f.).

Who May Accompany the Birth-worker?

Previously there was no statutory provision about this in Norwegian law; it was for the hospital to decide. There has been an increasing tendency in the Scandinavian countries to allow the father of the child to be present (NU A 1980:17, clause 6.1). The research available shows that it is of much more importance than was previously assumed for the woman to have somebody with her at the birth. In a study where fathers had participated in preparatory birth courses, the results clearly showed that the birth-worker had fewer pains and received noticeably less medication if the father was present all the time (NU B 1979:10, p. 84f.).

Research shows however, that it is not always entirely positive for fathers to participate during the birth. The father may react negatively or be disgusted: the birth may even be traumatic for him. The birth-worker may feel the man's presence to be problematic because he is negative, not very participative, or faints. Some men distance themselves from the birth by filming or taking photographs (NU A 1980:17 clause 2.3 cf 6.1).

In the Children Act the mother's right to have somebody with her during the birth is laid down in s.2: "At the birth, the mother has a right to be accompanied by the father of the child or somebody else who is close to her, if this is not inadvisable for medical reasons."

From the birth-worker's point of view, the history of the draft of the Children Act is interesting. Section 2 originally read as follows: "The person who claims to be the father of the child has a right to be present at the birth unless the mother is opposed to this or it is inadvisable for medical reasons." This provision laid down the father's right to be present, not the birth-worker's right to have somebody with her. Her legal position was formulated as an exception to the father's right, and her right to have others present was not mentioned in the Act.

In the relevant Bill, section 2 was amended out of consideration for the protests made during hearing. The Norwegian Feminist Organization, for instance, stated that the rule should

> be changed so that it expresses the woman's right to have somebody she wants present during the birth. A birth is such a special situation that it must be the woman's right that is emphasized, and this should be directly expressed in the wording of the Act. Such a rule will also enable women to have somebody they know with them if the child's father cannot or will not be present during the birth. It may also be the case that the woman wishes to have somebody other than the father of the child present. The woman's wish should be conclusive (Ot. prp. no. 1 (1979–80):11).

This is in line with the Danish Parents and Birth Organization's demands and is also similar to the comments from a Finnish birth institution: "the idea of a less conventional birth has brought men into the birth institutions without investigating the women's view of this" (NU A 1980:17, clause 6.1).

Further Details of the Birth Help

The obligation to give birth help also means that the help must be of a certain standard: it must be professionally competent. The prelude to the Medical Practitioners Act states in section 27 (about immediate aid):

> The help that the doctor is obliged to give, is that which is needed in the situation. But it may be the case that the doctor should not restrict himself to what is necessary at the moment, but give the complete treatment that is natural, with subsequent advice and instructions. The doctor who is summoned to a woman in labour, to a seriously injured person, to a child with high fever, should give all the help that is natural to give, with subsequent advice and instructions (Ot. prp. no. 1 (1979–80):236).

The Medical Practitioners Act contains an express provision concerning competent medical practice (s.25):

> "A doctor is obliged to practise his profession competently. He shall do his best to give his patients skillful and careful help."

As a legal safeguard, it is reassuring that the obligation is now expressly laid down in the Act. A closer definition of what is "competent" is, however, not easy to give: the concept is vague. The Act will, no doubt, primarily apply to gross and obvious cases of neglect. It is necessary to be more specific. What does birth help actually mean? I will concentrate on two questions. Firstly: Can health personnel intervene in a normal birth against the birth-worker's will? Secondly: What guidance are health personnel obliged to give in connection with the birth?

Initially, one is clearly protected against interference by the provisions of chapter 22 of the Penal Code – even in hospitals (Andenæs 1971:43–48). All types of injections, anaesthetics or narcosis are initially regarded as physical assaults and cannot be forced on anybody.

As regards what analgesics are commonly used today, and the principles for their use, I will refer to a manual entitled *Pregnancy, birth and babycare*, published by a private concern and, "written by medical experts". The book is distributed free in Norway and Sweden.

The following analgesics can, for instance, be given during a birth:

* *Laughing gas*: the birth-worker can use it herself when she needs it.
* *Analgesic or sedative injections*: They must not be given too early, so that the force of the contractions decreases, nor too late, so that they restrict the child's breathing.
* *Back anaesthetics*: (epidural anaesthesia) Gives full anaesthesia during the dilating and expelling period. The squeeze contractions can be weakened a little. Specially qualified narcosis personnel is required. The use of this method has become steadily more widespread.
* *FDP (paracervical blocking)*: This anaesthetizes the nerves around the cervix through an injection in the vagina. The contractions must be strong and the child must not have shown any sign of lack of oxygen.
* *Pudendal blocking*: Is used during the expulsion and anaesthetizes the vagina and the perineum. The squeeze contractions are not affected.
* *Local anaesthesia*: of the perineum can be done with a spray or injections.
* *End narcosis*: is a rapidly effective narcosis that kills pain for about 1/2–1 minute. It can be given when the head of the embryo has come so far that the midwife can finish the birth without any more pushing on the mother's part. Specially qualified narcosis personnel is required.

As regards the principles for their use, the following example may be given:

How far one can go in the use of analgesics mainly depends on the following:

1. The mother must be able to participate actively in the birth. This means that she must neither be terrified by pain, nor heavily affected by sedatives.
2. All sedatives, painkillers or narcotics penetrate the placenta and pass into the embryo. If the child has difficulties in adjusting to life outside the womb, the effects of a drug can be an extra burden. In the adaptation after the birth, the child should be "awake" and in the best possible form. The effects of a drug last longer in a newborn child than in the mother. This is mainly because the child's ability to break down and excrete drugs is not yet fully developed (Saba A/S 1978:52–58).

Even if all types of interference are initially unlawful, the birth-worker may legitimize them by her *consent*. In the case of more serious interference consent alone will not provide sufficient justification: it must be combined with *medical indication*. If complications occur during the birth, the staff's opinion is conclusive. In this instance they have a statutory obligation to intervene as defined in s.387 of the Penal Code:

> Any person is liable to fines or to imprisonment for up to 3 months who fails, although it was possible for him to do so without special danger or sacrifice for himself or others
> 1. To help any person who is in immediate and imminent danger to his life ...

Such cases are excluded in what follows: Here interventions in births with a *normal* course, are dealt with. It is then essential to decide *what requirements for consent are to be made*.

If the birth-worker expressly and unambiguously states that she does not wish the intervention to be carried out, the staff must comply with her wishes. If the birth-worker has neither objected nor consented to the intervention the general rule is that consent must be obtained before any intervention can be carried out: "The mental condition of the person giving consent must be such that he understands the scope of the act and can evaluate its significance" (Andenæs 1971:48).

A birth will normally be fatiguing, demanding and often a dramatic experience for the woman. The pains are continuous; she cannot enter into discussions. If the consent is to have any real meaning, she must have discussed the birth with the staff beforehand. She does not know of course how the birth will go in practice. But given the many good courses on preparatory birth work that constantly emphasize psychoprophylaxis, many women will have definite opinions about what kind of birth they want. They need help and support from the staff to manage this. Psychoprophylaxis is a detailed training program that is rehearsed before the birth so that the woman has learnt to meet the contractions with active breathing and relaxation. She is acquainted with the course of the birth in detail and knows how to meet the different phases with breathing and physical relaxation. The different kinds of painkillers all have side effects. Any wish on the woman's part to use as few of these as possible should be respected and supported. In this connection the above-mentioned study in which the presence of the child's father resulted in the woman needing markedly less medication is of interest. This shows that the effect of support and encouragement can be just as favourable as that of the painkillers.

The conclusion is that if consent is to have any real meaning, the woman must be enabled to discuss the birth beforehand. If she starts off by refusing painkillers, her consent must, of course, be obtained during the course of the birth, and painkillers must not be forced on her. The person whom the woman wishes to have with her during the birth should be allowed to be present during the preparatory talks, if the woman so wishes.

Finally, I would like to say something about *interventions for the purpose of research*. Extensive research activity takes place at hospitals. The woman may be offered painkillers or, for instance, given the opportunity to be induced (artificial inception of the birth) in order to gather material for a study. This may in itself be a good purpose, because it will be of benefit to birth-workers.

From the legal point of view, however, it should be a prerequisite that the birth-worker knows that this too is the purpose of the intervention and that she gives her consent on this basis. Here, the ordinary rules about physical assault are applicable. If the birth-worker is aware of the circumstances and gives her consent, the action becomes legitimate in terms of the Penal Code s.235 (Andenæs 1971:47).

Guidance and Information

There is a clear connection between the requirements for consent and the need for guidance and information. The birth-worker and the person whom she wishes to have with her have a great need for different kinds of guidance and information. Before the birth, information is needed about the course of the birth and about one's own situation (e.g. the position of the embryo and whether the pelvis is too narrow) and furthermore, information about the current routines of the maternity ward. Practice shows that in some places, "teaching visits" are provided for the parents (NU A 1980:17, clause 6.1).

Furthermore, throughout the birth good continuous information is needed about how it is progressing (about the size of the opening and whether the embryo sounds are good). The birth-worker's active co-operation depends on such information. After the birth, detailed information about the child is the main need.

How the staff shall inform parents of a handicapped or stillborn child is dealt with in detail in a preliminary report. There is, for instance, a guidance plan for the staff about how they best can help the parents. The valuable ideas presented here will also to a great extent be applicable to the general guidelines in the confinement ward (The Information Committee for the Handicapped Child 1979). The guidance/information given in different wards around the country varies greatly in practice, with regards to its content and form. This is partly a neglected field, partly a field that can be difficult for the staff to cope with: "In the ward the pressure of work is often great. Practical duties, administration, report writing and meetings take a lot of time. There is little time and surplus energy for contact with the patients. Some do not consider this work important, so that the situation becomes awkward for those who find it important and necessary."

The working conditions in the ward can also create difficulties. Sometimes there are no clear agreements about who is responsible for certain tasks. This can easily lead to uncertainty; one does not assume responsibility oneself, but believes instead that others will. This sometimes prevents parents from getting the necessary information and help. "Defective information about the parents' situation makes us unprepared for the parents' needs, and it is easy to leave them to themselves. Problems often occur if the parents ask questions, because we do not know what others may have said. The result is that we answer evasively or refer to others, feeling at the same time that we are letting the parents down." The Information Committee 1979, see NU A 1980:17 and St. meld. no. 32 (1976–77). Legal safeguards in social and public health institutions:47.

Section 25(2) of the Medical Practitioners Act prescribes the duty to give information: "He (the doctor) shall give each patient such information as he should have about his state of health and treatment. The doctor shall, as far as possible, allow the patient to participate in the treatment."

This is a *duty* that the doctor has and consequently a *right* for the birth-worker; she *shall* have guidance/information even if she is not a patient in the ordinary sense: Pregnancy and labour are not diseases. In the prelude to the Act it is pointed out that it is not necessary for the doctor to give the information himself: He/she is only responsible for the patient "getting information that he shall have, in a suitably satisfactory way and with understanding and tact. This he must control."

As regards the *contents* of the guidance information the prelude to the Act states:

> The doctor shall see to it that the patient gets not only information in the ordinary sense about the fact of the case, but also what one often calls medical advice. This may include purely medical and hygiene matters, but it will also go further and include life and diet, work and education, relations with other people, family, friends, workmates and neighbours (Ot. prp. no. 1 (1979–80):100f.).

From this it is evident that the duty to give information is quite extensive. The need for information that the birth-worker (and perhaps the other person present) has before, during and after the birth, clearly comes under the statutory provision, which undoubtedly covers much more than this.

The Routines of the Confinement Wards – A Legal Evaluation

What right has the management of the institution to decide for those who are admitted there? The basic legal principle is that one needs legal authority to "encroach on the citizens' legal sphere" (the principle of legality). Another formulation used by Eckhoff is: "no one can bind himself or others by legal dispositions or decisions unless he is competent to do so. And if there is no other basis of competence, legal authority is needed" (Eckhoff 1978:143).

Competence may be defined as "*an ability*, for instance, to bind oneself or to decide for others by making laws, pronouncing judgments, making administrative decisions etc. . . . to fulfil certain conditions that the legal system lays down for the recognition of dispositions or decisions in question" (ibid:123).

What basis of competence does the institution's management have for prescribing the routines for the confinement wards? It has no direct legal authority to prescribe such routines. But by virtue of proprietary powers, the owner will have a right to make decisions within the institution, if such powers are not limited by various kinds of rules (see further discussion).

Norwegian hospitals are subject to different forms of proprietorship. They are partly owned by private persons, the municipalities, county municipalities (in most cases) and the state. In practice, every hospital has developed its own routines – which to some extent vary a great deal. Has the owner got a free hand, or are there legal limits to what the routines may include?

Staying in birth and confinement institutions is formally voluntary (even if birth at home is not an alternative for most women today). Eckhoff considers that there is a legal contractual basis for mutual rights and obligations between the institution and its clients:

> A basic condition for staying in an institution is that one subjects oneself to the special communal standard resulting from having many people living close together and sharing common day rooms and common housekeeping. This entails, for instance, that one must put up with having meals at certain times, and that silence may be demanded in the house at the time of the day when most people want to rest. What other routines one must obey, will depend on the purpose of the institution.... Obligations beyond those that are a consequence of the inmates' staying in an institution of a particular type cannot be imposed without legal authority (ibid:162).

The last part of the quotation is in line with a principle that is being increasingly acknowledged and has been emphasized in a number of recent public announcements: the rules must not restrict the patients' self-expression to a greater degree than is justified by the purpose of the stay in the institution.

The purpose of the stay will therefore set a limit to what the owner can decide by virtue of this private proprietary right. What then is the purpose of the stay in a confinement ward? Previously, it had to be assumed that the purpose was mainly to protect the mother and the child's *physical* health, as well as to prevent infant mortality and puerperal fever.

Today the importance of mental health has also been increasingly emphasized: The WHO's concept of health covers this; psychological research has the same emphasis: for instance, a fourth stage has been added to the birth process, namely integration of the family. In the Scandinavian study of confinement, the different objects are summarized as follows:

> Today three basic goals of the assistance given to mothers around the labouring process are: 1) to increase the safety for mother and child; 2) to avoid unnecessary pain, without the loss of positive and ecstatic experiences; and 3) to establish a framework that will create a basis for a harmonious relationship between mother and child and father (NU B 1979:10, 74f., NU A 1980:17 clause 2.4).

As regards the last objective, the results show that parents can be together with their child to a varying degree. Few fathers have facilities for looking after the child where such facilities exist at all. There are still places where fathers can only see their child through a window pane (in Norway in 10 per cent of the institutions).

As regards the mothers, it appears from the published guidelines that some places operate with "rooming-in", other places with fixed breastfeeding and care times. The material gives insight into the great variations there are between the institutions' routines. In some places the routines seem unnecessarily strict and almost obstructive of any contact between parents and child. Accordingly, they seem partly to conflict with what should be the purpose of the stay (NU A 1980:17, clause 6.3; see the Ministry of Health and Social Affairs 1978: Breastfeeding in Norway).

On this basis criticism must be aimed at routines of this type. As mentioned above, the voluntariness of the admission to the hospital is largely a fiction. One must travel to the closest maternity home/ hospital or wherever one is directed. To a great extent an actual monopoly situation exists and there are limits to what a monopoly can lawfully impose upon one (Eckhoff 1978:163).

For the sake of comparison as regards children in hospital, the Ministry of Health and Social Affairs has drawn up guidelines (dated April 1979) which deal with parents' and children's rights to be together. Confinement stays are just as important for the family and also concern nearly all families with children.

Parental Responsibility

It may be asked whether parental responsibility (previously parental authority) does not limit the proprietary power. In the Children Act it is defined in s.30: "The child is entitled to care and consideration from those who have parental responsibility. They have a right and a duty to make decisions for the child in personal matters within the limits prescribed in sections 31 and 33. Parental responsibility shall be exercised in the child's interest and to meet the child's need."

In the comments on s.30 it was stated: "The duty to show care and consideration for the child will be especially extensive during the first years of its life."

Nothing is expressly stated about the relationship between a child in an institution and parental responsibility. In the preparatory works to the Children Act it was, however, generally stated: "parental authority is a fairly exclusive right for the parents, when confronting others who for one reason or the other wish to decide for the child. This is expressed in s.26 of the Penal Code, which provides penal protection: Any person who unlawfully removes children under 18 years of age from their parents' care or authority is liable to imprisonment for up to 3 years" (NOU 1977:35, p.45).

It must be assumed that parental responsibility commences from the birth of the child: the Act makes no exception, and in ss.30, 35 and 36 of the draft of the Children Act this is clearly assumed (ibid. pp. 158, 122). Any confinement routines that prevent the parents from exercising care and consideration for the child conflict therefore with the statutory parental responsibility.

Own Decisions in Birth Institutions

In St. meld. no. 32 (1976–77) concerning legal safeguards in social and public health institutions, protection against being rendered legally powerless was emphasized as a central aspect. Fair and considerate treatment of individual cases must be guaranteed. One must be allowed to participate in a decision that concerns oneself. In cases in which such participation is not wholly possible, the reason for the decision should be explained to the person concerned. In administrative law Eckhoff describes this as follows:

> ... the person concerned is given status of a party. This means that he shall not be regarded as an object which the administration can deal with arbitrarily, but as a competent subject who shall be informed of the matter at issue and be allowed to defend his interests ... so that one is not reduced to a nonentity (Eckhoff 1978:91).

The principle of self-determination in birth law is a specification of the general requirement of specification of legal safeguards.

To what extent do the rules protect one against being rendered legally powerless in birth institutions? The regulations concerning birth institutions are characterized partly by defective legislation and by very general legislation (e.g. the Medical Practitioners Act, the Penal Code, the Hospital Act). The only thing that is clearly established is the right to *get* birth help and the right to *have* someone *with* oneself at the birth. Furthermore, minimal information about the rules applicable is given. Almost none of the information leaflets or books that are distributed to the pregnant/confined women mention their legal position in the maternity and confinement wards.

These circumstances – general, defective legislation and lack of information about it – will of course reduce the rules to paper provisions. As regards the important consent rules, for instance, the woman is not aware of them, and secondly, many women have no contact with the hospital beforehand, so that the necessary preliminary talks cannot take place.

What often happens in practice is that the woman arrives at the maternity ward in a great hurry with pains and contractions. Here she meets an experienced staff of strangers, surrounded by professional equipment. In such a situation she has little possibility of establishing her rights, especially when these rights are so unclear on many points. As it says in the above-mentioned information booklet: "The birth doctor in consultation with the child doctor and the narcosis doctor must decide which painkilling method is most suitable" (Saba A/S 1978:54).

The birth-worker's rights are here completely suppressed. Not even the midwife is asked for advice. Legally the guarantee against being rendered powerless is minimal. If the woman gets good birth helpers and comes to a good confinement ward, everything will be all right. If she does not, there is not much she can do about it.

The report concerning legal safeguards is not specially concerned with birth and confinement wards, but it does mention a closely related field – children in hospitals. In this regard the special problems created by the separation of children from their parents are recognized. The considerations are much the same as in the relationship between parents and the newborn:

> ... it has been shown that the stay in hospital can have serious harmful effects on the child as a result of the separation from the parents. The question therefore arises whether one ought not to have regulations that secure small children certain rights during

their stay in hospital, as well as benefit rules that will enable parents to stay together with their children in hospitals (St. meld. no. 32 (1976–77):47).

In guidelines from the Ministry of Health and Social Affairs of 2 April 1979, it is stated in clause 1, paragraph 1: "If the child is under six years of age or if there are other special circumstances, a close relative should be permitted to be together with the child night and day for the first five days after admittance to the hospital and/or after surgery." (See also the National Insurance Act, ss.3-22, which gives the right to financial benefit when a child is ill.)

From the point of view of legal safeguards, more precise rules concerning the birth help and routines should be evaluated and drawn up. Furthermore, the rules should contain *real*, not just formal rights. Information about such rights should be included in the usual preliminary birth information, and arrangements should be made, so that the pregnant woman and her family can make good contact with the institution beforehand.

Planned Home Birth and Other Alternatives

Legally speaking, women have a right to give birth at home. According to the former Midwives Act, the midwife was bound to come to "women in labour, without delay" unless she was prevented from doing so because she was giving birth help to somebody else or if she was ill (former Midwives Act, s.84). Section 2-4(2) of the National Insurance Act fully reimburses expenses incurred for help from midwives and doctors (see Medical Practitioners Act, s.27) in connection with birth and pertinent illness. In addition, a birth benefit is paid – a sum of money determined by Parliament.

In practice, a woman's right to carry out a home birth has been greatly reduced. In Norway, very few midwives are able to participate in home births because they are all tied to jobs at the maternity wards of health institutions, etc. Planned home birth has therefore become a rather unrealistic alternative today. Most women also prefer to give birth at an institution.

Many will ask whether there is any point at all in keeping the alternative of planned home birth. Is it not much safer and better to give birth at an institution? Is not this discussion obsolete?

It appears that there is an increasing interest in home birth as an alternative.[2] In Denmark, where better arrangements for home births exist than in Norway, a group of midwives have stated, in connection with their research project about planned home births:

> Our basic attitude is that IT IS SIMPLE TO GIVE BIRTH. What we want to achieve is that as many women as possible will experience giving birth – whether they give birth at home or in a hospital – as an event directly connected with the rest of their lives and their everyday existence, an event that they themselves and their families can influence (Gannik et al. 1982:2).

The Danish midwives are eager to show that it is *quite feasible* to choose home birth as an alternative today too, because pregnancy and birth are a natural process that the woman can manage perfectly well with the assistance of the birth-helpers. They maintain that home birth is not dangerous if the woman is well nourished and if she has been regularly examined by her doctor and midwife and if she is not in the risk group (e.g. if she is diabetic or if the child is lying in the wrong position). Accepting home birth as normal puts the birth-worker in a central role, in contrast to the institution births where the birth-worker must adapt herself to the system and thus easily accept a passive role and lose confidence that she can give birth herself.

This is a complicated and emotional subject. Many will resist the idea of home births, especially professional people and women who have experienced sudden complications during the birth. But regardless of what one thinks, most women today wish to give birth in institutions. It is not very likely that this development will be reversed to a noticeable degree, one reason being that birth at home today differs from what it was in the olden days when the woman had her relatives, her servants and her neighbours around her for help and support. The woman's immediate environment must therefore also be adapted to home births.

Both legally and practically speaking, women in Norway today thus have very little choice. The fact that birth-workers have different needs has not been taken into account. Some wish to give birth in a central institution with specially qualified doctors, and others wish to give birth in a small maternity ward closer to home or to give birth at home. Some wish to be moved to a smaller maternity ward in their neighbourhood after the birth is over. Some wish to go home early, perhaps only a couple of hours after the birth; others want to stay at the institution for a week or two, to feel secure in the new situation. This is important for giving the family a good start, but is not taken into account either in the legislation or in practice. The birth-worker must be included in the birth legislation as the central person and be given the right to make real choices.

The Birth Experts and the Woman

The old-time wise women, who gave advice and help throughout the process of birth, have today been replaced by a motley crew of "birth experts": pregnancy control at the doctor's, preparatory birth courses with the physiotherapist, maternity wards with one staff, confinement wards with another, public health clinics for infant control, again with experts who are strangers. This is a problem for all families during this phase of life, but especially for those who do not have others to rely on.

The birth process is divided into many phases, instead of being treated as it is – *an entire process*. As is stated in another Danish report on midwifery:

> ... money is spent on experts and specialists instead of personal comradely support and help. There are sharp borders between the professional groups and about one's own field, instead of willingness, pleasure and time to learn from or listen to each other. An external belief in authority and a desire for professional loyalty to those most highly qualified within the system is predominant, which is detrimental to the client's rights, and it often happens that the ordinary pregnant belly is touched by the hand of 10 to 20 different strangers, and that the woman herself is expected to listen respectfully to the different opinions of the 40 or so professional people she is attended by. Pregnancy and birth have become a sort of disease that requires treatment (Gannik et al. 1982:97–98).

In suggesting new strategies, it is stated as a conclusion:

> in short that the hygiene of pregnancy and the birth help should be planned in accordance with the fact that a pregnant woman is a sensitive, feeling and emotional creature, who can most suitably be understood and "treated" by a limited number of other persons' open minds and skilful hands, instead of a crowd of strangers, who to a great extent rely on machines and apparatus (ibid:99).

Midwifery has long traditions: it is one of the oldest professions for women. It has existed all over the world and in very old cultures (among the Egyptians, the Babylonians, the Romans, the Greeks, the Chinese, the Incas). Obstetrics has come a lot later. The midwives' training included the whole process of the birth.

Today most Norwegian midwives are employed in maternity wards. The course of development is tending to put them more and more in the background. The anaesthetists, for instance, are getting more say, because of the increasing use of painkillers. The midwives I have been in contact with regard this as an unsatisfactory development. They have a strong need for better and longer contact with the pregnant/confined woman and her family. They also wish to work outside the hospitals, and to give a greater degree of guidance. They want direct links between the birth and confinement wards, not separate units, as is usually the case today. They wish to come in contact with the woman beforehand, for instance by having the pregnancy check-ups in the hospitals, or by running pregnancy check-ups at the public health clinics themselves. Where there has been contact between the midwife and the birth-worker beforehand, the general experience is that the birth has been a lot easier.

These, I think, are important ideas. A pregnant woman needs a stable contact who can follow her through the whole birth process. This will make it possible for her to participate in decisions about the birth process herself and to plan the birth to a far greater extent.

It is obvious that the midwife is the person best suited for this task, with her special training as a birth helper and with her attitude that it is a natural process. It is therefore important that the midwife's rights and duties are clarified and laid down in the coming legislation. Midwives must be given further duties – also outside the hospitals – so that they are not absorbed into the hospital hierarchy in the ranks of children's nurses and ordinary nurses. In those countries where midwifery has disappeared, for instance in the USA, women have afterwards organized illegal midwife groups to give each other birth help and to get midwifery reinstated in the long run. Scandinavia is, for instance, pointed out as a model.

Birth law has until now been marked by controlled legislation (the termination of pregnancy legislation, legislation about unmarried mothers), whereas legislation conferring rights has been very poorly developed. The special protection provisions in working environment and social security legislation are inadequate and, as we have seen, provisions conferring rights are too few in the public health legislation. Now is the time for the birth-worker and her family to get positive rights, to make their own birth preparations, to get guidance, to be given a choice of the place of birth and method of birth and to have stable contact with a midwife throughout the birth process, including the months after the birth.

Notes

* This article was first published in Tove Stang Dahl (ed.), *Kvinnerett II.* Oslo: Universitetsforlaget, 1985.

1 Because of great geographical distances there are a large number of births on route to an institution in Norway, see NU A 1980:17, p. 257.

2 Personal communication with the headmistress at the National College of Midwifery, Berta Berg, 13 May 1982.

3

Stillbirth and Parents' Legal Rights*

KIRSTI STRØM BULL

Introduction

In Norway the only clearly stated legal rights in relation to childbirth are the right of a woman to have with her the father of the child or somebody else who is close to her (the Children Act s.2), and the duties imposed on doctors (the Medical Practitioners Act s.27), and midwives (the Midwives Act s.5) to give assistance to women in childbirth and on hospitals to receive women in labour (the Hospital Act s.6).

There are duties on doctors and midwives to act in a creditable way, i.e. "He shall do his best to give his patients competent and careful help" (the Medical Practitioners Act s.25(2) and the Midwives Act s.3) and to obtain her informed consent to any practice requiring consent, for example administration of anaesthetics or pain relief, surgery, manipulation (the Medical Practitioners Act s.25(3)): "The doctor shall give each patient the information he should have about his state of health and treatment. The doctor shall, as far as possible let the patient participate during the treatment."

However, the exact meaning of this law in practice is unclear. For instance, to what extent do medical personnel have to inform pregnant women of the options for anaesthetics before labour and ascertain their preferences? Is consent given during labour at a time of anxiety, confusion and possibly fear, a real consent?

Such rules touch only on a small aspect of the childbirth process. Today it is recognized that it is important for mother and child to be together after the birth and not to be separated, so that the natural bonding process may take place. It is also realized that contact between father and child, and the introduction of the child to any brothers or sisters is very important. However, there are no written rules that take care of the need for information of both mothers and fathers before, during and after the birth. Nor is anything laid down which guarantees the necessary contact between the child and mother, father and siblings (Fastvold 1985).

The need for information and for contact with the child is generally recognized in relation to children whose birth is normal, who are healthy and well-shaped. Often forgotten are the unhappy occasions when birth does not follow the normal pattern and the child is born dead or dies shortly before birth. For those special births we also need written rules to take care of families' needs. In this paper I want to look at the practice of hospitals in relation to stillbirth (a term which in this paper only includes children born dead, not those who die shortly after birth) and the rights parents have in relation to stillbirth. I shall look at the right to information, contact and help, rights of leave from paid employment and income support, and the right to burial. Drawing on empirical research done in 1982 and 1984 in sixteen towns in Norway, I shall argue that hospitals need to be aware of the local practice of burial of stillborn children in order to fulfil their duties of help and information towards the patients. Moreover, I shall argue that these burial practices and the rules on which some are based need to be changed.

The Right to Information and Help

Current Practice

The information and help that are given to the parents who have a stillborn child probably vary from one maternity ward to another. Some wards are well aware of the help that the parents need, and I will here, as an example, show the routines at Kongsvinger Hospital (Nilsson 1980). As soon as possible after the birth, the mother, possibly also the father, is given the opportunity to see the dead child. Some will refuse, but the offer will be made again some days later. It is also possible for the parents to see the child several times. The parents are given extensive information on the cause of the death. The mother will often reproach herself concerning incidents that occurred during pregnancy which she thinks may be connected with the stillbirth, but which have been without significance. At this maternity ward the staff are anxious to try and get such misunderstandings out of the way. During the stay in the maternity ward, the question of burial is discussed with the parents. All parents involved wished to have the child buried in a known place, often in a family grave. The mother is allowed to have her closest relatives with her day and night immediately after the birth. The mother may also have daily talks with the personnel about what she has been going through, and through these conversations she also gets help to prepare herself for the situation after she is discharged. At this maternity ward they also followed up with talks with the parents after the mother had been allowed home. If necessary, a health visitor is contacted.

However, in other maternity wards, the attitude to problems concerning stillbirth is often different. The opinion is that it is best for the parents not to be confronted with the dead child, and that they should try to forget what happened as soon as possible. It is not uncommon for the child to be removed soon after the birth, and that no offer will be made to the parents to see the child or to take part in the funeral. The information provided often concerns the cause of the child's death. It also happens that a quick decision is required regarding the burial of the child. The parents then often find themselves in a situation where they cannot manage to take a considered and helpful decision and they choose what they often feel may help them to forget the birth as soon as possible, namely a very anonymous burial.

From my own experience, I am in no doubt that the parents who have a stillborn child need the information and help offered at Kongsvinger Hospital. Literature on the subject shows that parents who have a stillborn child experience just as much grief as others who lose one of their loved ones: "The depth of the grief does not depend on whether the child lived at the birth. For some perhaps a stillborn child releases even more intense grief reactions, partly because what was lost was the experience of holding one's own warm living child in one's arms" (Wretmark 1979).

It is important that the grief is given an outlet, and that one can go through a normal mourning process. If not, the feelings can develop into a pathological grief, accompanied by mental sufferings. The parents often need help to be able to get accustomed to the shock which the stillbirth represents. In this connection it is important that the stillbirth is not made into a non-experience, but that the parents can feel that they have been parents – parents to a child they have lost. They should therefore be allowed to see the child and they should be given a real choice concerning the burial. Such choice can only be made after having received appropriate information from the hospital staff. It is a widespread belief, however, that the parents have never known a child who dies at birth, and so they have no reason to grieve; it is therefore best for them not to be confronted with their dead child. This understanding is clearly in conflict with more recent, extensive literature on the subject, where the need for an outlet for the parents' grief after a stillbirth is strongly emphasized.[1]

The Duties of a Maternity Ward

If the parents ask for information, ask to see the dead child and ask to take part in the burial, the ward has a duty to fulfil all these wishes. According to the Medical Practitioners Act s.25(2) and (3), a doctor has a duty to give his patients "competent and careful help" and to give "each patient the information he should have about his state of health and treatment". Even if a birth is not a disease, a woman in labour must clearly be considered as a patient. The literature listed in the notes following this chapter shows that it is of great importance to the mother's mental health that she gets information about the child and has a right to see it. As a patient she must therefore, in accordance with s.25 of the Medical Practitioners Act, be entitled to information not only about her own condition but also about that of the child, and she must have a right to see the child.

The father cannot be regarded as a patient. But he is the child's relative, and his right to information about the child follows from the Medical Practitioners Act s.26. According to this rule, relatives shall – when circumstances so permit – receive information about the patient's state and disease and about the treatment. Both the wording and the statements in the *travaux préparatoires* are aimed at the cases where the patient lives, but the doctor's duty of information also applies when the patient is dead.

According to the "case history decision", the right to information also follows from ordinary principles of law.[2a] Rules on the running of hospitals are contained in the Act relating to Public Administration of 10 February 1967 and regulations as to the duty of information are also contained in s.11 of the Public Administration Act, which imposes on the administrative body an ordinary duty to give guidance.[2b] According to Professor of Law Asbjørn Kjønstad (1982), the relationship between doctor and patient may be considered a contractual one, and a duty of information follows from the doctor's contractual obligations.

In line with the studies that have been used as the basis for the "case history decision", the parents must also have a right to see their dead child and to decide about the burial.

In the judgment mentioned, it is stated that such information as dealt with in s.19 of the Public Administration Act is exempted from the duty of information; this may be information which it is inadvisable to convey, for instance out of regard to the person's health. In the event of a stillbirth, it is possible that the parents may be denied information or not allowed to see their dead child out of regard for the parents' health. But such refusal can only be accepted in special cases; it is usually best for the parents to get as much information as possible. Also where the child is born with severe handicaps or has been dead for some time before birth, it is recommended that the parents be allowed to see the child (Wretmark 1980).

In the case where the parents ask for information, want to see the child and ask to be allowed to decide about the burial, the conclusion is therefore clear: The hospital has a duty to comply with all the wishes. But usually the parents do not ask for this. Often they are so shocked over what has happened that they cannot bring themselves to ask for anything at all – perhaps apart from the cause of the child's death. All existing literature on stillbirth recommends that the maternity ward should unsolicitedly inform the parents and help them to let their grief out. In this connection it is important to invite the parents to see their dead child, and to take part in the funeral. But is it the duty of the doctor or the midwife to do all this when the parents do not ask for it?

According to s.25(2) of the Medical Practitioners Act, a doctor shall do his best to give his patients competent and careful help. Such duty also rests on midwives pursuant to s.3(2) of the Midwives Act. According to literature on the subject, the best help a doctor or a midwife can give is to teach the mother how to let out her grief. However, it is still a widespread understanding that it is best for the mother not to be confronted with the dead child and not to be tormented with questions about the burial. As there seems to be disagreement among doctors as to what is supposed to be the best form of help in these circumstances, one may hardly say that the doctor has a duty to help the mother deal with her grief, especially if he himself believes that advice should not be given unless asked for. As appears from the literature mentioned above, grief reactions in connection with stillbirths have not been a big subject in Norwegian literature. Much more attention has been paid to the subject abroad, and what has been published is fairly new. Against this background, a doctor or a midwife *today* probably has no duty to deviate from existing practice in the maternity wards. However, literature on this subject is increasing, and we must therefore expect that the subject will attract more attention in Norway too. It is therefore only a question of time before the maternity ward, according to s.25 of the Medical Practitioners Act and s.3 of the Midwives Act, will have a legal duty to give more active help to the woman in her efforts to deal with her grief when she has had a stillborn child.

The needs of fathers for information and contact cannot be extended from existing law in the same way. As a relative, his rights are regulated in s.26 of the Medical Practitioners Act, but one can hardly, with reference to this rule, impose a duty on the doctor to help the father in his grief unless he is invited to do so. Nor does a midwife have such a duty under the Midwives Act.

Even if theoretically we would be able to decide that, according to the Medical Practitioners Act and the Midwives Act, a doctor or a midwife should have a legal duty to help the parents of a stillborn child without being asked, this would not be of much help unless an actual change were made in the routines of the maternity ward. The Information Committee for Handicapped People of the Ministry of Social Affairs took the initiative to publish a guide for health personnel on how to assist families having a handicapped, sick or stillborn child. The Committee proposed at the same time to draft guidelines as to how health personnel could help such families. A booklet, entitled *There is something wrong with the child* has been published, but apart from that, nothing has happened (Kvisli 1983). Different training schemes for health personnel were to be started, and leaflets were to be produced, but nothing has been done. Nor have guidelines been issued for routines in maternity wards. Such routines were proposed in Part 3 of *There is something wrong with the child*, but the efforts came to nothing. The Committee which took the initiative has now been dissolved.

Norway has a higher rate of perinatal deaths than the other Scandinavian countries. This prompted the Directorate of Public Health in 1983 to set up a committee to assess measures designed to improve the work in the health sector in connection with pregnancy, birth and newborn babies. The Committee's recommendation, called *Perinatal Care in Norway – Health Care Amongst Pregnant Women and Newborn Children* (NOU 1984:17) primarily discusses the technical aspects of the help. Unfortunately, the care of and information to parents having a stillborn child were not included in the committee's assignment. However, to quote an English article on stillbirths: "there is more to neonatal care than simply the technological aspects of management" (Davies 1983). It is gratifying, however, that care of and help to relatives in connection with a stillbirth is mentioned in the recommendation from the committee that was set up at the same time, and which was commissioned to consider "nursing and care of seriously ill and dying people" (NOU 1984:30, pp. 39–40).

Different Rights in Connection with a Stillbirth

According to the Working Environment Act s.31, a woman has a right to eighteen weeks leave in connection with pregnancy and birth. Twelve weeks leave can be taken during pregnancy and after the birth she must take at least six weeks. In connection with a stillbirth, a woman might possibly wish to go back to work before the end of the six weeks, and in that case she has the right to do so provided it is stated in the doctor's certificate that it is best for her to go back to work earlier (cf. the Working Environment Act, s.31, No. 1(3)).

However, if the woman wants leave exceeding six weeks after the birth, she may have another twelve weeks, provided these have not been used during pregnancy.

The leave in connection with pregnancy and birth under the Working Environment Act is leave without pay. But according to the National Insurance Act, a woman who has been in work is entitled to a maternity benefit. The maternity benefit is usually the same as a woman's wages and is granted for thirty-three weeks (as per 31.12.92). Maternity benefit can be paid for twelve of these weeks prior to the confinement. If the child is stillborn, she is entitled to maternity benefit for six weeks after the confinement. But if she has not used the right to maternity benefit before the confinement, she has no right to such benefit beyond six weeks.

Under a collective bargaining agreement, the woman may be entitled to leave with pay beyond the period stated in the legal rules referred to here.

The father is entitled to two weeks leave in connection with the birth to help the mother, and he has this right also if the child is stillborn (cf. the Working Environment Act s.31 no. 2). He is not, however, entitled to paternity benefit or other kinds of compensation for lost wages during this leave unless laid down in the collective bargaining agreement.

The maternity benefit as a rule corresponds to the mother's wages, see the National Insurance Act, s.3-21 no. 1(3) and s.3-4. If the mother has had no income, or a very small income, the maternity benefit is paid as a lump sum, cf. the National Insurance

Act, s.3-21 no. 6. As of 31.12.92 the amount is NOK 14,825 for each child.

A single mother gets a supplementary maternity benefit, cf. the National Insurance Act, s.12-2 and s.10-3(3). As of 31.12.92 the supplementary benefit amounted to NOK 10,470 for each child, and is granted also when the child is stillborn.

Stillbirths have to be registered in the population register in the place where the mother resides at the time of the confinement, see s.8 of regulations issued by the Central Bureau of Statistics of 26 November 1979,[3] and the child may be given a name in the register.

The Right to Burial

Stillborn children are always buried, but the manner in which this is done varies from one place to another. In order to find out more about the general practice, I applied in 1982 to the churchwardens in Oslo, Bergen, Trondheim, Tromsø, Drammen, Tønsberg, Bærum and Kristiansand and asked the following questions:

1) Are stillborn children buried in a common grave or in the grave of an adult?
2) Can the parents, if they so wish, get a grave of their own for the stillborn child?
3) If the child is buried in a common grave or in the grave of an adult, can the parents be shown the place where the child is buried if they should wish to see it later?

I received answers from all, except the churchwarden in Kristiansand, and they gave the following information:

1) All, except Drammen and Oslo, answered that stillborn children were buried together with an adult. In Drammen and Oslo they were buried in a common grave. In Trondheim, the plan was to use a common grave.
2) Tønsberg said no. Drammen stated that there had never been a request for a separate grave. Tromsø and Bærum answered yes. Bergen and Trondheim referred to their regulations stating that one could not demand a separate grave for a stillborn child. In Trondheim, however, it was possible for the stillborn child to have a grave of its own if the parents so wished. In Bergen, stillborn children could have a separate grave if failure to grant their wish would lead to mental problems for the parents. Oslo

gave the same answer as Trondheim, but without mentioning that churchyard regulations in Oslo decide that stillborn children have no right to a grave of their own.

3) All churchwardens answered that if the child was buried together with an adult, the parents could not later be shown the place. In Drammen, they could be shown the area where the stillborn children were buried, but not the exact place. In Oslo it was possible for the parents to see the place where the child was buried.

In order to find out whether practices had changed, I sent a new inquiry to the same municipalities in 1984, and I also applied to the churchwardens in Bodø, Fredrikstad, Hamar, Lillehammer, Molde and Stavanger. I also sent the questions to the vicar of Tynset and the sexton in Flora[4], two small towns in Norway. The 1984 answers were as follows:

1) Lillehammer, Bærum, Bodø, Tønsberg, Kristiansand, Fredrikstad, Bergen, Tynset and Stavanger stated that the child was buried in the grave of a randomly chosen adult. This is also the case in Hamar, but most stillborn children are cremated and the ashes are placed in a common memorial grove.

In Molde, stillborn children are buried in the grave of an adult provided the relatives of the adult consent. If not, the child is buried in a grave of its own. In Flora the child is not buried in a randomly chosen adult grave, but in a family grave or in a grave of its own.

In Oslo, Drammen, Tromsø and Trondheim, there is a memorial grove for stillborn children, and they are buried in a common grave.

2) Fredrikstad, Tromsø, Trondheim, Kristiansand, Oslo, Bærum, Bodø, Lillehammer, Hamar, Tynset, Stavanger and Drammen stated that the parents can have a separate grave for the child. In the churchyard regulations for Oslo and Trondheim it is stated that stillborn children shall not have a grave of their own, but if the parents wish it to be so, the wish may in practice be granted. In the churchyard regulations for Bergen it is also stated that stillborn children cannot have a grave of their own. In 1982 the Bergen authorities said that a separate grave might be found for the child, if it could be proved that the parents would otherwise have mental problems. Today, practice has changed so that no documentation of the parents' need is required. If the churchwarden gets a reference from a doctor or a priest, who on

behalf of the parents asks for a separate grave for the child, no further documentation is required.

From Molde it is stated that stillborn children have a right to a grave of their own.

3) Oslo, Bergen, Trondheim, Tromsø, Drammen, Bærum, Hamar, Bodø, Stavanger, Lillehammer and Tønsberg all answered that if the child is buried in the grave of an adult, the parents cannot later be told where the child is buried. In Fredrikstad and Tynset they do not know how to deal with a question about where the child is buried.

In Kristiansand there was also some hesitation in answering the question. But in an interview in the newspaper "Verdens Gang" on 16 October 1984, the churchwarden of Kristiansand stated that the parents had a right to know where the child was buried.

In Molde, parents will be told where the child is buried even if it is in the grave of an adult. But, as mentioned, burial in an adult grave will only take place with the consent of the adult's relatives. In Flora, children are, as mentioned, never buried in the grave of an adult, and the parents will therefore always be allowed to see the place.

In Oslo, Drammen, Trondheim and Tromsø, where there now are memorial groves for stillborn children, parents will always be shown the place.

As will be seen from the answers to the inquiries in 1982 and 1984, changes are occurring in the practices concerning the burial of stillborn children. In Tromsø and Trondheim there are memorial groves. Oslo too has marked the common burial place for stillborn children as a memorial grove. Apart from local practice as we have seen it in Molde and Flora, it is still usual to bury a stillborn child in the grave of an adult. This is an arrangement which I believe ought to be abolished, particularly as it prevents parents from knowing where their child lies. But in order to make changes, it is often necessary to understand the background of the current practice.

The present practice of burying a stillborn child in the grave of a randomly chosen adult is probably based on old traditions and the earlier view of the fate of unchristened children.[5]

Before the Reformation, unchristened children had no right to be buried in consecrated ground. Since they had not received the redeeming gift of grace inherent in baptism, they could not have eternal life. Unchristened children were not members of the church and could therefore not be buried in consecrated ground. Even though the view of the salvation of unchristened children changed after the Reformation, the old doubts about the fate of unchristened children remained for a long time. And although we no longer believe that unchristened children will meet with a worse fate than others, old customs and traditions have survived. An example of this is emergency christenings.

While pre-Reformation Christian law contained rules stating that unchristened persons had no right to be buried in the churchyard[6] there are no rules on the burial of unchristened persons either in The Norwegian Law of 1687 or in Denmark's and Norway's Church Ritual of 1685.

The Church Ritual of 1685 did, on the contrary, contain a regulation that an unchristened child is also a child of God: "If such a child dies in the womb or before it can come to christening and Christianity, without the parents being in any way at fault or negligent, then they have a good conscience and can rest assured that it is a child of God" (Smith 1823).

However, there are still rules in the Church Ritual of 1685 that reflect the old view of baptism as being necessary for the salvation of the child; see Chapter II, Article 1, where it is stated that the mother herself can baptize a newborn child who is "in mortal danger", when there is no time to call anybody else, and where it is said: "If it then dies, it has been well christened, because it has received the true baptism, about which the priest teaches the mother, so that she shall by no means be in doubt."

After the Reformation, recommendations stated that unbaptized children could be buried in the churchyard "propter spem resurrectionem, without, however, the presence of the sacristan, the ringing, singing by the boys and other cermonies". In later recommendations in the 17th century it is stated that the ceremony of sprinkling earth on the coffin could take place if so wished by the relatives. This must apply to fully developed children, however, not to aborted babies.

From Olav Bø's article "Boxes in the Church Wall" it appears that stillborn babies were buried without the assistance of the priest. Either the parents themselves lowered the coffin into the grave of an adult; or this was done by the midwife. In many places the sexton helped to bury the child. The burial took place in secrecy, unless the child was buried together with an adult relative who died at the same time. Then the burial could take place more openly.[7]

It looks as if stillborn children hardly ever got a grave of their own. There may be different reasons for this practice. When an adult died at the same time, it may have been considered more practical to bury the child together with the adult. In many places it was also looked upon as positive for an adult to be buried together with a child. This practice may also be evidence of the idea that one did not want the child to lie alone.[8] But this burial custom may also be due to the fact that a stillborn child never lived, never became an individual, and therefore it was not natural for these children to have a grave of their own. I think practice is primarily rooted in the old view of unbaptized children. Infants that die shortly after birth are often buried in the grave of an adult, even if they have lived. Even if we no longer believe that unbaptized children suffer a worse fate than others, baptism is still important as a social rite of integration. At the christening the child gets a name and a name gives the child an identity.[9] Without an identity, the child could have no grave of its own in the churchyard.

This is clearly expressed by the Finnish social anthropologist Juha Pentikäinen (1968): "A name was the most important symbol of status long before the advent of Christianity. If the child has not belonged to the community of the living, he cannot be incorporated among the dead. Burial rites are either not performed at all or are performed in a special way. The child who has died without a name is regarded as an 'outsider', who is not granted membership of the group of the family dead. The situation somewhat resembles that of a stranger who has died. There is no group that considers it its duty to care for the dead person's status in the after-life."

That the christening was a condition for the infant's right to a grave of its own was also expressed as late as 1975 in a statement by the meeting of Norwegian bishops: "When a child born alive dies in the hospital after the birth, the death shall be reported in the usual way. As a rule the child has then also been baptized. In principle, this means that the child is entitled to a grave of its own."[10]

More about the Rules on Burial of Stillborn Children

According to s.9-1(3) of the National Insurance Act, a women who has a stillborn child has a right to a funeral grant. While funeral grants according to the first paragraph are paid at a fixed rate, grants according to the third paragraph are paid only to cover necessary expenses, but the amount is not to exceed the rate pursuant to the first paragraph.[11] In accordance with a circular issued by the National Insurance Administration, questions as to what are necessary expenses shall be decided following a concrete assessment of each separate case. The National Insurance Administration has decided that expenses for a wreath (or flowers costing approximately the same) from the parents and the expenses for an announcement of the death in one newspaper may be covered. Expenses for a tombstone may also be covered. A funeral grant may also be paid where the child is buried in the grave of another person.[12]

According to Article 16 of the Constitution, the King shall make provisions concerning matters of the church, including burials. In a regulation on funerals, approved by Royal Decree of 27 February 1981, general provisions, item 5, it is stated: "Where a funeral is wanted for a stillborn child, the rites will be limited to the sprinkling of earth on the coffin" (cf. II, A, 12 (II, B, 9)). There can be no ordinary funeral from the church or chapel. The reference to point 12 in II, A and to point 9 in II, B, means that only a plain sprinkling of earth on the coffin can take place, and there will be no blessing, no singing of hymns or ringing of bells.[13] This also used to be the practice according to the *Altar Book for the Norwegian Church*: "At the burial of stillborn children, the short version of the ceremony shall be used."[14] Thus, the burial of stillborn children shall still take place "without the ringing of bells, singing by boys and other ceremonies". Yet, it must be possible to hold a short ceremony at the bier, as described in the funeral regulations III, A.

As we have seen, it is not unusual for churchyard regulations to contain a rule stating that stillborn children have no right to a grave of their own. But, is it possible for the churchyard authorities, by referring to the regulations, to deny parents a separate grave for their stillborn child? The churchyard regulations are issued by authority of the Churches and Churchyards Act s.42(3). Here it is stated: "Otherwise, general regulations on churchyards and the use of them, including the placing and removal of memorials, benches, plants, fences, hedges etc. shall be given by the supervisory body, with the approval of the chief supervisory body."

Today the Parish Council functions as supervisory body and the chief supervisory body is the Diocesan Council. The text of s.42(3) indicates that the delegation of authority only concerns the practical aspects of the administration of churchyards, and that the delegated authority does not cover the right to give rules as to who shall have a grave. Since the Reformation, the church has recognized the right of stillborn children to be buried in consecrated ground. Even though the practice has been to bury stillborn babies in the grave of an adult, I fail to see how one today can deny stillborn children a grave of their own only with reference to the regulations. If so, this would have to be made statutory. As my inquiry will show, neither in Oslo nor in Trondheim would a stillborn child be refused a grave of its own, regardless of the regulations. This shows that it is not self-evident that stillborn babies have no right to a grave of their own.

The Right of the Relatives to Later Be Shown the Place of Burial

As my inquiry discloses, today parents will probably not be shown where their child is buried if it lies in the grave of an adult. Nor will the parents be shown the exact place if the child has been laid in a common grave, they will only see the area. This is because it is not known where the child is buried. According to the Churches and Churchyards Act s.38(2), exact records shall be kept of all the graves in a churchyard, and this is the responsibility of the Parish Council, see s.47. Regarding the registration of the burial places of stillborn children, practice varies from one place to another.[15] If they are buried in the grave of an adult, the place is usually not marked, and it is therefore not possible to find the grave. This may also be the case if there is a common grave; this is marked, but there is no information as to which child lies where.

However, even if the churchyard authorities know where the child is buried, they refuse to show the parents the place. Where the child is buried in a common grave together with other stillborn babies, I fail to see how the authorities can refuse to show the place, not even if this should be laid down in the regulations. For many people, knowing where one's next-of-kin is buried is a fundamental need, and there can be no weighty considerations against showing the place to parents when the child is buried in a common grave.

If the child has been buried in the grave of an adult, the parents' wish to know where it is may conflict with the wish of the adult's relatives that "their" grave may be left in peace. Furthermore, the owner of the grave can often refer to churchyard regulations stating that no one must be buried in a grave owned by someone else without consent.[16]

But a breach of these rules does not give the churchyard authorities a right to refuse parents to be shown the grave. As said before, one human fundamental need is to know where one's next-of-kin is buried; and where the parents have not themselves chosen a burial where they know that it will not be possible later to find the place, they will feel hurt by not having the right to know. In this case, however, the need of the parents must be balanced against the wish of the owner to have "his" grave for himself. I have no definite opinion as to how these two interests should be balanced against each other.

What has been stated above shows that the practice of burying stillborn children in the grave of an adult must come to an end. The parents' wish to have a separate grave for their stillborn child must be granted. Where the parents have no such wish, and where they do not wish to have the child buried in a family grave, the stillborn baby should be buried in a common grave for stillborn children. Thus, the parents may – if they later should so wish – be shown the place where the child lies. Moreover, the Ministry of Church and Education should inform maternity wards as to the practice concerning burial of stillborn babies. Today there is little knowledge about these questions. Knowledge of how stillborn children are buried is necessary in order to provide the parents with proper information, so that they will be able to make a real choice concerning how they want their child to be buried.

Notes

* This article was first published in Tove Stang Dahl (ed.), *Kvinnerett II*. Oslo: Universitetsforlaget, 1985.

1 Johan Cullberg, Reactions towards perinatal child death (I): Mental consequences for the woman. *Läkartidningen 63*, pp. 3980–86; Reactions towards perinatal child death (II): The Relationship Patient-Doctor. *Läkartidningen 63*, pp. 4065–68. Ulla Berg and others: Information and support to parents who have lost their child at the birth. *Läkartidningen 75*, pp. 128–32. Emanuel Lewis: Mourning by the family after a stillbirth or neonatal death. *Archives of Disease in Childhood 54*, pp. 303–6. Michael Clarke & Anthony J. Williams: Depression in women after perinatal death. *The Lancet* (1979), pp. 916–17. Larry G. Peppers & Ronald J. Knapp: Maternal reactions to involuntary fetal/infant death. *Psychiatry 43*, pp. 155–59. Ronald I. Clayman and others: Issues concerning parents after the death of their newborn. *Critical Care Medicine 8*, pp. 215–18. Astrid Andersson Wretmark: Death before life has really started. *Läkartidningen 77*, pp. 4042–45. Kari Kvisle & the Information Committee for the Handicapped (1983): *There is something wrong with the child*. Oslo. (2nd edition 1983) (In Norwegian). Gillian C. Forest and others: Practical management of perinatal death. *British Medical Journal 282*, pp. 31–2; Support after perinatal death: A study of support and counselling after perinatal bereavement. *British Medical Journal 285*, pp. 1475–79. D. P. Davies: Support after perinatal death. A study of support and counselling after perinatal bereavement. *British Medical Journal 286*, pp. 144–45. Liz Standish: The loss of a baby. *The Lancet* (1982), pp. 611–12. Bo Lindberg: Parents' relations after perinatal death. *Jordmodern 96*, pp. 5–14 (In Swedish). Bitten Munthe-Kaas: *When the child dies before life starts*. Oslo 1985 (In Norwegian).

2a A patient who had been treated in a public hospital demanded to see his case history, which the hospital refused (referred to in Rt. (The Norwegian Law Journal) 1977.1035). The patient was given the right to see the papers, and the decision was based on general legal principles. A decisive factor was the patient's need for information and legal guarantee. The right to see the case history is authorized in the Medical Practitioners Act s.46 and the Midwives Act s.8, but the decision is also of principal interest so far as the general rights of patients are concerned.

2b See also Rt. 1977.1035, particularly on p. 1046.

3 The regulations are authorized by Royal Decree of 16 January 1970 in accordance with the Act on Population Registers of 16 January 1970. The rule stating that stillbirths shall be registered in the population register was introduced at the amendment of the regulation on 25 October 1982. Before that, stillbirths were not registered in the population register.

4 It is in itself an interesting observation that in the municipality of Flora, it was the sexton who could provide the answers. The vicar's office did not know. This shows the connection with previous practice when the stillborn child was buried without the assistance of the church (see below).

5 The following is to a large extent based on Olav Bø (1960): Øskjer i kyrkjemuren (Boxes in the church wall). *Norveg*, pp. 99 et seq.; Bjarne Hodne (1980): *Å leve med døden* (Living with death). Oslo; Arne Bugge Amundsen (1983): *Dåp og tradisjon* (Baptism and tradition). Oslo.

6 Cf. *Gulatingslov* Chapter 22, *Eidsivatingslov* I, Chapter 2 and Archbishop Jons *Christian Law*, Chapter 16.

7 There is reason to believe that there have been local variations concerning the burial of unchristened and stillborn babies. In Skjærstad in Nordland, for example, there seems to have been more openness about the burial of these children. Sometimes they were even allowed to have a grave of their own. The information is provided by Astri Riddervold. See also the practice in the municipalities of Flora and Molde.

8 Older people providing information in the municipality of Skjærstad expressed this view when talking to Astri Riddervold.

9 Amundsen, op. cit. pp. 41 et seq.

10 The minutes from the meeting of bishops, November 1975, item 27. Burial of children who die immediately after the birth. The meeting proposed to the Ministry that guidelines ought to be established "ensuring a uniform practice as regards the burial of children who die in hospital after the birth. They are registered, and are entitled to a grave of their own." In connection with the same item it is said about stillborn children that they "shall be placed in a grave together with another bier".

11 The rate is determined by the Storting and as per 31.12.92 amounts to NOK 4000.

12 Circular from the National Insurance Administration of 29 December 1979 Kom./Sak 09-00; pp. 2–3.

13 The funeral regulations II, A contain the liturgy for sprinkling earth on the coffin. The funeral regulations II, B, contain the liturgy for sprinkling earth on the coffin in the crematorium and, exceptionally, in the church or chapel.

14 *Altar Book for the Norwegian Church*:155. Prior to 1920 the rule also applied to unbaptized children.

15 In Kristian Hansson's book on Norwegian church law it is stated: "When burial of a stillborn child is wanted, it is usually placed in the grave of a relative or in another grave. Such burials are not entered into the church register of deaths. There are no further rules on registration, but it may be deemed reasonable to enter the burial of a stillborn child in the churchyard protocol or register." (*Norsk kirkerett*, Oslo 1957, pp. 141 et seq.).

16 An example of this is the churchyard regulations in Bergen, s.15(2).

4

The Right to Self-determined Abortion*

RAGNHILD OLSNES

Introduction

Self-determination is a fundamental consideration in birth law, and in 1978 the persistent demands of the feminist movement for self-determined abortion were a long way on the road to being met through amendments to Act no. 50 of 13 June 1975 concerning the Termination of Pregnancy (The Abortion Act). As a general rule, during the first twelve weeks of pregnancy a woman has the right to have her pregnancy terminated if she so wishes.

The right to termination of pregnancy has gradually been extended. Norway adopted its first Abortion Act in 1960, and according to this Act an Abortion Board was responsible for deciding applications for an abortion. Prior to 1975 a woman had neither an independent right to apply for an abortion nor to appeal against a decision. A doctor had to act on her behalf. Today, as a rule, the woman has sole responsibility for the final decision as to whether or not she shall terminate the pregnancy, as long as she makes her decision before the end of the twelfth week of pregnancy (the Abortion Act s.2(2)). After the twelfth week of pregnancy has elapsed she is still required to apply to a Board to terminate her pregnancy (s.2(3) and s.7(2)). Thus, the situation has developed from an almost complete lack of independent decision under the 1960 Act to a limited right to participate in the decision in the 1975 Act, including an independent right of application and appeal, and hence to a right of self-determination before the end of the twelfth week of pregnancy according to the 1978 Act (the Act implementing amendments to the 1975 Act).

After a brief review of the development of abortion law, I will discuss the rules in the current Act, focusing in particular on the conflicting interests which arise in the interpretation and practice of the law: women's interests, legal protection of the foetus, professional interests, economic interests, etc.

The History of Legislation on Termination of Pregnancy[1]

Before 1960

Up to 1960 cases of termination of pregnancy were regulated by the Penal Code. Section 245 stipulated that a woman could be punished with up to three years in prison for the illegal termination of pregnancy (feticide), and anyone aiding and abetting in such an act could be imprisoned for up to six years. In principle, termination of pregnancy was illegal unless the pregnancy constituted a serious risk to the woman's life or health – in other words: in principle, induced abortion was both illegal and a punishable offence. In practice, it was the doctor who drew the distinction between legal and illegal abortion, because a termination of pregnancy carried out by a doctor was not usually considered illegal.

The number of operations increased steadily during the period between the two World Wars and after the Second World War. This was partly due to developments within the health sector, including hospital building and better medical knowledge and technology, and partly to a more liberal view of abortion both among doctors and in society as a whole. At the same time there was also a strong increase in the number of illegal terminations of pregnancy. Our knowledge of this fact is based partly on the increasing number of women who were admitted to hospital to be treated for injuries caused by illegally induced abortions. The numbers were as shown in Table 4.1.

It goes without saying that the situation for a woman applying for termination of pregnancy was very uncertain, and varied depending on where in the country she lived, and what kind of doctor she came into contact with. Katti Anker Møller, in her famous lecture in 1915, was the first to speak up for liberalization of access to terminate pregnancy, and to maintain that induced abortion should

Table 4.1. Registered and illegal abortions in Norway 1920–1954.

Registered – "legal" abortions	Illegal abortions
1920: 115	about 600
1933: 1822	about 2300
1949: 2049	about 5550
1954: 3157	about 7300

Source: Ot. prp. no. 15 (1959) concerning the Act relating to the Right to Terminate Pregnancy.

no longer be regarded as a criminal offence on the part of the woman. The lecture led to intense public debate, but to no change in the legislation. The next step was when doctors raised the question of termination of pregnancy at the annual meeting of the Norwegian Association of Surgeons in 1929. The debate flared up again – and there were marked differences of opinion, not least among the doctors themselves.

Specifically, the initiative taken by the doctors led, in 1934, to the Ministry of Justice asking the Criminal Law Commission to consider the question of a special Act to regulate termination of pregnancy. The committee submitted its recommendations in 1935 (First Recommendation of the Criminal Law Commission relating to Amendments to Section 245 of the Penal Code and relating to the implementation of an Act relating to Termination of Pregnancy). In brief, the recommendations were that a woman could be granted an abortion on medical and ethical grounds (rape and "incest"), and on the basis of hereditary and social considerations, and that the matter should be decided by a Board of doctors. The proposed legislation, in particular the part referring to social indications, was strongly opposed. For this reason, the recommendation gave no concrete result. After long discussions, the Ministry finally returned the matter to the Criminal Law Commission for further consideration. The Second World War interrupted debate on this matter, and no new initiative was taken until 1951, this time as a result of strong pressure from feminist organizations. The gap between law and practice had also become so wide that there was an obvious need for clarification. The Ministry of Justice again asked the Criminal Law Commission to consider the question of a special Abortion Act.

The 1960 Act (The Act concerning Termination of Pregnancy in Certain Cases of 11 November 1960, No. 2)

The recommendation from the Criminal Law Commission relating to the Right to Termination of Pregnancy was submitted in 1956, and became the basis for the first Abortion Act. The purpose of the Act was to establish more specific rules and more uniform practice among doctors, and to reduce the number of terminations of pregnancy which, in the Council's opinion, had become far too large. The proposal from the Criminal Law Commission in 1956 was very much the same as presented by the Criminal Law Commission in 1935, and was again a matter of intense debate. In spite of this, it was adopted with only few changes.

The Act defined three reasons for termination of pregnancy. The proposal of a special social indication was removed during reading in the Storting. Instead, the medical indication was extended, in conformity with developments in the field of social medicine. The indication explicitly expressed that an application for termination of pregnancy should be considered on the basis of a total evaluation of the woman's physical and mental health. This was in line with the standpoint of the Norwegian Medical Association, which was that an abortion should be granted for medical reasons only. This made doctors the only persons competent to decide applications for termination of pregnancy. The other two indications were the hereditary indication, that is to say, a woman could be granted an abortion if there was risk of the child developing a serious injury or disease, and the "ethical" indication, which said that the woman could be granted an abortion if she had become pregnant from intercourse with a close relative or after being raped, or if she were insane or mentally retarded.

In order to be granted an abortion a woman had to apply to an Abortion Board through a doctor. Only if the woman was "considerably mentally retarded" (s.4) could any other person than herself submit the application. As a rule, if she was a minor or was mentally retarded the parents could express an opinion, and if she was married the husband could do so. The doctor was expected to "sieve" the applications, that is to say, he was expected to send the application to the Board only if he thought there were grounds to terminate the pregnancy. If the application was refused, the woman could similarly only appeal if the doctor who had submitted the application on her behalf agreed, and in this case, the application was forwarded through the County Medical Officer to another Board. Illegal termination of pregnancy was still a punishable offence.

The Act did not come into force until 1 February 1964. The reason for the delay was that it was first necessary to build up a system of support for pregnant women in a difficult situation, but this was not done.

The Abortion Act did not lead to fewer terminations of pregnancy, nor to equal conditions for women who applied for an abortion. The number of applications for an abortion increased from 4715 in 1965 to 16,052 in 1974.

The number of applications that were granted increased from

73.3% in 1965 to 94.5% in 1974, but varied from Board to Board. In 1974 the proportion varied from 88.2% in the county of Troms to 97.7% in the county of Telemark (Ot. prp. no. 38 (1974–75):37, 40).

The fight about abortion therefore continued. Many wanted to see a more restrictive practice – and an increasing number wished to liberalize the access to terminate pregnancy. The different treatment experienced by different women was strongly criticized. A woman applying for termination of pregnancy was still dependent on the doctor with whom she came into contact and, as mentioned above, there were great differences in the practices of the different Boards. The battle over abortion became more intensive with the growth of the feminist movement in the early 1970s. The demand for self-determined abortion was raised in earnest – and an "Anti-abortion Movement" was founded.

The Women's Branch of the Labour Party managed to get self-determined termination of pregnancy included in their party's agenda, and in St. meld no. 51 (1973–74) concerning the Standard of Living of Families with Children the Labour Government proposed to introduce self-determined abortion up to the end of the twelfth week of pregnancy.

The 1975 Act (The Termination of Pregnancy Act of 13 June 1975, No. 50)

There was not a majority in the Storting for self-determined termination of pregnancy, but a new Act was proposed and adopted which led to a major improvement on some points at least. Termination of pregnancy was no longer a criminal offence on the part of the woman. Certainly, s.245 of the Penal Code had been dormant for many years – but it had still existed. Furthermore, the woman obtained the independent right to apply for an abortion, and to appeal, that is to say, the right to demand that the doctor whom she contacted send her application to a Board. Moreover, appeal became automatic unless the woman actively withdrew her application. The indicative basis for termination of pregnancy was extended. The proposition on which the Act was based, Ot. prp. no. 38 (1974–75) on an Act concerning Termination of Pregnancy, included only a proposal for a social medical indication, in line with the rule in the 1960 Act. During discussions in the Storting the social medical indication was considered as a separate item, and was finally approved as grounds for terminating the pregnancy. Another important change was that the wording of the Act was such that if the Board found that one or more indications for an induced abortion were present, the woman had a *right* to an abortion. Nevertheless, the Storting did not wish to impose a similar obligation on the individual doctor, and introduced a legal right to make reservations. Doctors and other health personnel were given the right to refuse to carry out or assist in operations leading to termination of pregnancy. It was the duty of the county health authorities to ensure that the woman's rights were served. A last important point was that the age limit for when the parents of a pregnant girl had the right to express an opinion was reduced to 16 years, and the husband's right to do so was withdrawn. Thus the 1975 Act placed much more emphasis on women's interests.

The liberalization of practice with regard to abortion continued, and in 1977 as many as 97.2% of the applications were granted, although the percentage still varied from Board to Board. The primary Board in Østfold granted an abortion to 91.3% of the applicants, while in Telemark the percentage was 99.2% (Ot. prp. no. 53 (1977–78): 18, 20). The battle over abortion still continued. Gradually, a united feminist movement supported the demand for self-determined termination of pregnancy, and won more and more persons to their point of view.

In 1978 we at last experienced the amendment to the law which, in principle, gave women the right to self-determined abortion up to the end of the twelfth week of pregnancy (Act no. 66 of 16 June 1978 concerning Amendments to the Termination of Pregnancy Act of 13 June 1975 No. 50). After the twelfth week, a woman still has to apply to a Board for an induced abortion, and the indications are the same as before.

The debate on the abortion legislation did not end with the introduction of self-determined abortion. Anti-abortionists are still active. In St. meld. no. 17 (1982–83) on Experiences with the Termination of Pregnancy Act, and Measures to Prevent Pregnancy, the minority Conservative Government proposed introducing compulsory ethical advice for women applying for an abortion, but the proposal did not obtain a majority in the Storting.

Thus the current law is Act No. 50 of 13 June 1975 with the amendments adopted in Act No. 66 of 16 June 1978 (hereafter referred to as the Abortion Act). By authority of s.12 of the Act, the Ministry of Health and Social Affairs has prepared Regulations for the Implementation of the Act, laid down by Royal Decree of 1 December 1978 (hereafter referred to as the Regulations). In addition, the Ministry has published an information brochure, entitled "The Act concerning Termination of Pregnancy, with amendments, regulations and guidelines". This is not a source of law in the ordinary sense of the term, but is an important source of information on how the law is practised. The brochure is intended for persons without legal qualifications who have to deal with applications for termination of pregnancy and/or carry out or assist in operations to terminate pregnancy.

Termination of Pregnancy Before the End of the Twelfth Week of Pregnancy

The Main Rule: Self-determined Termination of Pregnancy

Before the end of the twelfth week of pregnancy the main rule today is that a woman has a right to an induced abortion if she herself so wishes (s.2(2)):

> . . . she shall herself make the final decision concerning termination of pregnancy provided that it is possible to perform the operation before the twelfth week of pregnancy has elapsed . . .

Therefore, at such an early stage of the pregnancy, it is the woman herself who has the right to decide, and she is not required to justify her decision to terminate the pregnancy to any other person.

The Procedure

The woman must submit her application for termination of pregnancy to a doctor (the primary doctor) (s.5(1)). If the woman has not formulated a written application for termination of pregnancy herself, the doctor has a duty to help her to do this (s.1(2) of the Regulations).

The doctor examines her and determines the duration of the pregnancy. He/she also has a duty to provide the woman with information (s.5(2)). In brief, this information is of three different kinds: Medical information, which is obligatory, and information on public assistance and ethical advice, both of which shall be offered to the woman. After the doctor has informed the woman in accordance with these rules, he has a duty to refer her as soon as possible to an institution where the operation can be performed (ss.3 and 6(1)). At the institution the woman will be examined again and "the medical superintendent or his deputy" (hereafter called the hospital doctor) finally determines the duration of the pregnancy (s.5 of the Regulations). In practice, the hospital doctor will be the doctor who is to perform the operation. Provided that no rules of exception are applicable, the operation is then carried out. The hospital doctor is responsible for ensuring that the operation to terminate the pregnancy is performed as soon as possible (s.5(2) of the Regulations).

More Details About Information and Advice

One of the controversial issues in the debate on abortion was what kind of information and how much information and advice a woman should receive before an operation to terminate pregnancy. Many of those with a restrictive view of abortion believed that the woman should receive extensive counselling and guidance prior to a possible termination of pregnancy. It should not be "a simple matter" to terminate a pregnancy, and to counteract this impression it should be compulsory to have detailed talks with the woman about the possible consequences, other solutions and ethical issues. The advocates of self-determined abortion were sceptical about rules concerning information and advice to women applying for an abortion. Women who had applied for an abortion could tell of humiliating treatment by doctors and Boards, and in hospital. Pro-abortionists were afraid of rules which could be used to legitimize unreasonable influence and pressure. It was feared that when the doctors no longer had the formal authority to make the decision they would be tempted to retain control by frightening the women applying for an abortion. The result was that information on the nature of the operation and its medical effects is *obligatory*, but information on the assistance offered by society and other advice should be a *service*, i.e. should be provided if the "woman so desires" (s.5(2)).

According to s.5(2) the woman has a right to be told how the operation will be carried out, and about any possible consequences of the operation. The right of the woman corresponds with the doctor's duty to provide this information. The fact that this information is obligatory is evident from the wording of both the Act and the travaux préparatoires to the Act (Ot. prp. no. 38 (1974–75): 21, Ot. prp. no. 53 (1977–78): 15). A general duty to provide information has now been established in the Medical Practitioners Act s.25, based on the same considerations: A patient has the right to be informed about his/her state of health and about the treatment he/she will receive. The provision in the Abortion Act is also justified on the grounds that the woman must receive this information in order to have an adequate basis for a decision to terminate the pregnancy.

According to the travaux préparatoires, the doctor shall give a "general orientation", in line with the information everyone should receive prior to medical treatment. In other respects, the detailed content of the information is decided by the individual doctor. It is emphasized in the Guidelines that the information should be "realistic and objective, and should neither be alarming nor make light of the situation". To understand this somewhat surprisingly detailed specification, it is necessary to consider the way earlier Abortion Acts were practised, and the debate preceding the amendments in 1978.

The doctor shall offer to provide the woman with information on the public assistance to which she is entitled if she decides not to terminate the pregnancy (ss.5(2) and 2(1)).

In the proposition preceding the 1975 Act it was also proposed that this type of information should be obligatory. The reason was that a woman who wants to terminate her pregnancy should know "what this implies and what alternatives are available" (Ot. prp. no. 38 (1974–75): 21). A majority of the Parliamentary Committee on Social Affairs proposed that this proposal be changed, which is what took place. As mentioned above, during the debate preceding the amendments to the Act in 1978, some of the anti-abortionists again proposed compulsory information on measures of public assistance, but did not succeed in getting their standpoint adopted on this occasion either.

The question of ethical counselling has been very controversial. The rule that now applies was incorporated into the Act in 1978, after strong pressure from the opponents of self-determined termination of pregnancy. The Act merely states that the doctor shall offer the woman "advice so that she herself is able to make the final decision" (ss.5(2) and 2(1)). Neither the wording of the Act nor the travaux préparatoires define what is meant by the word "advice", but there is little doubt that this rather vague formulation refers to so-called ethical counselling.

It is stated in the travaux préparatoires that the ethical counselling shall help the woman to reach the solution which she feels to be best both in the short and the long term, and that pregnant women in a difficult situation can often be helped by "surprisingly moderate means, e.g. just ordinary human contact, closeness and understanding". It is not very clear what this implies. The most definite statement that is made is that the woman should "consider the seriousness of terminating life" (Ot. prp. no. 53 (1977–78): 15). On the other hand, the woman shall not be subjected to pressure (St. meld. no. 17 (1982–83): 35). We know that people have strong and conflicting views about abortion. Ethical counselling would depend very much on who provided it, and their ideology and sense of values. The risk of influence and prejudiced and condemning advice still exists. Instead of this kind of vague rule about advice, the Act could ensure that women who apply for an abortion are offered a meeting with one or more professional persons: a psychologist, a social worker or any other person whom she may wish to contact.

Rejection on "Serious Medical Grounds"

If serious medical grounds weigh against termination of the pregnancy, the woman's application for an abortion may be rejected. Only the hospital doctor has the right to reject an application for an abortion on medical grounds. This is made clear in The Abortion Act s.6(1) and the Regulations s.1. In other words, the primary doctor's handling of the case shall not be affected by this rule.

What is implied by the phrase "serious medical grounds"? The expression is defined in more detail in the Regulations s.6(2): "By serious medical grounds is meant conditions which are of such a nature that, due to the status of the woman, an operation must be assumed to present a serious risk to her life or her health." It is clear that the risk of injury must be greater than normal for such an operation, and similarly that the risk entailed by termination of pregnancy must be greater than the risk entailed by completing the pregnancy to term (cf. pages 24 and 26 of the Guidelines). The normal risk associated with pregnancy and birth is greater than the risk connected to an induced abortion (Ot. prp. no. 53 (1977–78): 12–13). Therefore we have to conclude that an application can be rejected in accordance with this provision only in very special cases. This is also underlined in the Guidelines. I have found no examples of somatic illnesses which can provide grounds for rejection of an application – it is stated in the Guidelines that such illnesses do not *normally* provide grounds for refusing the operation. The term must refer to mental injuries after an abortion. A number of studies have been carried out to discover possible mental injuries after having such an operation. It has not been possible to reach any certain conclusions. It is almost impossible to predict such injuries when these have to be weighed against the strain or injury which may occur if the woman has to complete the pregnancy to term (Grünfeld 1973. Cf. also Ot. prp. no. 53 (1977–78)). It is stated in the Guidelines that: "This will often be a matter of women who are strongly ambivalent towards the operation, who feel under strong pressure from the environment." It is possible to imagine a situation where the doctor has achieved good contact with the woman, and discovers that she herself does not really want to terminate the pregnancy but is being pressed to do so by someone else. However, in this kind of situation there is no need for any exception to the rule of self-determined abortion. Here it is not the woman herself who has made the decision and, for this reason, the doctor can reject the application. The fact that the doctor merely believes that the woman is being forced to apply for an abortion is not sufficient justification for refusing the application; what has been said above about assessing possible mental injuries in advance also applies in such cases. It is therefore difficult to visualize practical situations where it will be right to reject an application for termination of pregnancy in accordance with this rule.

Why do we have this rule then? This question is answered quite clearly in Ot. prp. no. 53 (1977–78): 15: "Self-determined abortion before the end of the twelfth week of pregnancy does not mean that the doctor's judgement and authority to make a decision is cancelled." Doctors are a strong professional group, who do not like their duties to be made too specific, and in many connections their professional interests have strongly influenced the legislation.

However, the Act does contain some kind of guarantee against this situation: If the hospital doctor "refuses to perform the operation for the reason that there are serious medical grounds to the contrary, the case shall be forwarded immediately to the County Medical Officer". The County Medical Officer shall ensure that the woman's application is considered by another institution, by another doctor (s.6(2)).

Special Rules for Certain Groups of Women

The right to self-determined termination of pregnancy does not apply to all women. In the case of women under the age of 16 years, mentally retarded women and women suffering from severe mental illness, ss.4 and 9 lay down special rules which affect the right of self-determination. The rules, as they are formulated today, are by no means clear – a result of the amendment to the legislation in 1978. The rules are the same as in 1975, and after the introduction of self-determined abortion before the end of the twelfth week of pregnancy ss.4 and 9 have other implications than before. There is one set of rules for persons under sixteen years of age and persons who are slightly mentally retarded, and another for persons who are mentally retarded to a considerable degree or suffering from severe mental illness.

Under Sixteen Years of Age or Mentally Retarded

According to s.4(1), the parents have the right to express their views concerning the abortion, unless there are particular reasons to the contrary. This right applies to "the person exercising parental rights or the guardian", which usually means the parents. According to the Guidelines, it is enough that one parent expresses his/her views (cf. also the use of the single person in the wording of the Act). When there are two persons who exercise parental authority, it is not stated which of them should have an opportunity to express an opinion. The reasonable thing would be to let the woman who is applying for the abortion decide.

The above is a matter of a right to express an opinion. The wording used in the Act is "shall be given an opportunity". The opinion is expressed to the hospital doctor (the Regulations s.5(5)). Therefore this rule shall not lead to changes in the treatment of the case by the primary doctor. There is reason to believe, however, that this does happen in practice. The Directorate of Health has prepared a form to be used by primary doctors for applications for an abortion (s.6(1)). This form, *I-1142*, requires the parent/guardian to sign a declaration that she/he is aware of the application and has received the information mentioned in s.5(2) from the primary doctor. This must be contrary to s.5(5) of the Regulations. In practice, this means that the primary doctor – not the hospital doctor – must decide whether an exception shall be made to the right to express an opinion, and whether he is then aware that this can be done. This is not made clear, namely, in the form. Further, the form includes an erroneous reference to the Act. Parents/guardians of all persons under sixteen years of age and all mentally retarded persons are requested to sign a declaration to the effect that they have received information from the primary doctor pursuant to s.5. According to the Act, it is only parents/guardians who have applied for termination of pregnancy on behalf of the woman (by authority of s.4(2), see below) who shall be informed about the nature of the operation and its medical consequences pursuant to s.5(2).

I assume below that the procedure prescribed in the Act is applied. If the parents do not choose to express an opinion, or do not express the view that their daughter should not terminate the pregnancy, or are not asked for their opinion, the rule has no effect on the right to self-determined termination of pregnancy. The hospital doctor can proceed according to the rules that normally apply. On the other hand, if the parents express the view that the pregnancy should not be terminated, then the provision in s.9(a or b) is applicable. In such cases the County Medical Officer must consent to the termination of the pregnancy. A normal linguistic interpretation of the wording of the law ("may be performed only with the consent of") implies that the County Medical Officer can refuse his consent. As mentioned above, in the travaux préparatoires to the amending Act of 1978, this problem is not mentioned, but there is a statement in the debate in the Odelsting on the 1975 Act to the effect that the member assumes that the doctor can refuse to grant the woman an abortion (Proceedings in the Storting, 1974–75: 420). A factor that weighs against the above interpretation is that an exception to the main rule of self-determined abortion before the end of the twelfth week of pregnancy should at least have been mentioned in the travaux préparatoires. Since these do not discuss the individual rules in any special detail, this is probably not sufficient reason for interpreting the rule in any other way than indicated by the actual wording. At the Directorate of Health the rule is also interpreted to mean that the County Medical Officer can reject the application (Conversation with M.B. Christofersen, Directorate of Health, December 1981). There are no direct guidelines for what factors the County Medical Officer should emphasize in his evaluation, probably because the rule was laid down with the Abortion Board in mind, before the principle of self-determined termination of pregnancy was adopted. However, for persons under the age of sixteen years, the rule in s.2(3d), applies. It is probably the case that, pursuant to this rule, all women under the age of sixteen years have the right to an abortion before the end of the eighteenth week of pregnancy. This means that s.9(a) becomes of formal value only, while s.9(b) may have a material influence. If the County Medical Officer rejects the demand for an abortion, there are no rules concerning the right to appeal etc.

There is one exception to the right of the parents to express an opinion, namely: "unless there are particular reasons to the contrary". As mentioned before, it is the hospital doctor who judges this situation (the Regulations s.5(5)). The expression "particular reasons" implies that, in any case, it shall not be the normal procedure not to obtain an opinion from the parents. Both in the Guidelines and the travaux préparatoires to the Act there is some discussion concerning what should form the basis of the doctor's judgement. Emphasis should be placed on "the woman's relationship to her parents, her level of maturity, whether she lives away from home, whether she is self-supporting, etc." (Guidelines: 32, see also Ot. prp. no. 38 (1974–75): 18).

Thus, two kinds of conditions have been conceived as particular reasons. The first is whether the woman is especially independent for her age, or whether the mental handicap has little or no influence on her ability to evaluate and take a standpoint on the question of termination of pregnancy. The second reason is whether the parents' knowledge of the pregnancy can create a poor relationship, or worsen the relationship, between daughter and parents. If the hospital doctor concludes that particular reasons do exist for not contacting the parents, then he need not do so. There is no rule stating that the County Medical Officer shall become involved in such cases. Thus it is the hospital doctor who decides the area of competence of the County Medical Officer. This means that, in these cases, the main principle still applies: the girl herself makes the final decision.

Today, the rules are not very well thought out. (Cf. the fact that they have not been reconsidered since the introduction of self-determined abortion.) A main principle of the Act was changed without reviewing all the rules in order to establish what other consequences the change would or should imply.

The right to express an opinion was introduced at the time as an obvious expression of parental authority. However, it has never been the case that the parents have had the authority to decide on behalf of their daughters as regards whether or not to terminate a pregnancy. It has always been taken for granted that the woman herself must request an abortion, irrespective of her age. The conflict has concerned where to set the age limit. In the Act of 1975 the age limit was lowered after some discussion from twenty to sixteen years. This age limit was maintained when the Act was revised in 1978. Only a few persons wished to strengthen the parent's or guardian's right to express an opinion. Their arguments are that the decision is so important that a young woman should not be asked to bear the responsibility alone, that parents should be told that their daughter is pregnant and wants to terminate the pregnancy, and that young women are particularly vulnerable to pressure. But, for this very reason, we must conclude that it must be up to the girl herself to decide who to confide in and ask for advice, before deciding what to do.

If a woman is "suffering from severe mental illness or is mentally retarded to a considerable degree", the parent or guardian may submit an application for termination of pregnancy on her behalf (s.4(2)). The woman's consent shall be obtained if "it can be assumed that she is capable of understanding the significance of the operation" (s.4(2)). If the woman has not given her consent, then the consent of the County Medical Officer must be obtained before the operation can be carried out (s.9(c)).

According to page 32 of the Guidelines, the term "suffering from severe mental illness" shall be interpreted in the same way as in s.5 of the Mental Health Act, and refers to diagnosed psychoses and certain mental states bordering on the psychotic. The term "mentally retarded to a considerable degree" refers essentially to persons with an IQ lower than 55, but assumes a total assessment. Before the amendment to the Act in 1978 it was clear that the Board was responsible for these evaluations. In the Act that now applies this is not clearly stated, but if the application for termination of pregnancy is considered by a Board it is still the Board that assesses the mental status of the woman. If the application is not handled by a Board, the responsibility lies with the hospital doctor. This conforms best with the other rules in the Act concerning medical responsibility.

If the woman consents to the abortion, can we then say that she herself has taken the final decision to terminate the pregnancy (s.2(2))? Section 4(2) does not give the parent/guardian the authority to make a decision concerning termination of pregnancy, only to submit the application. A termination of pregnancy which does not involve consideration by a Board depends on the woman herself taking a standpoint, cf. the wording in s.2(2) which concerns termination of pregnancy not involving consideration by a Board: ". . . *she shall herself* make the final decision ..." (my emphasis). It is not stated there that she herself must submit the application. This is regulated by s.4, and it is probably correct to interpret the Act in such a way that the application is submitted with the consent of the woman. The case will then proceed according to the rules which normally apply, except that it is the parent/guardian who shall receive the information in accordance with the rules in s.5(2). According to the wording of s.5(2), the woman herself has no right to receive information. It is stated there " ... *or* a person who ..." (my emphasis), but it is reasonable to assume that the woman has a right to information to the extent that she can understand it. The obligation to provide information pursuant to s.25 of the Medical Practitioners Act obviously also applies to such women.

If the woman objects to the termination of pregnancy – what then? This situation is not referred to either in the Act or in the travaux préparatoires to the Act, but the Act contains the term "consent" (s.4(2)), and to perform an operation to terminate pregnancy without the woman's consent is a serious matter, so serious that the authority to do so must be perfectly clear. It is obviously a problem, out of consideration for care of the child, to allow such women to give birth, especially when their closest relatives want them to terminate the pregnancy. But according to the Act this cannot be decisive.

If the woman is not capable of understanding what the abortion operation implies, her consent is not needed to carry it out. It has not been stated directly in the Act, and the question is not mentioned in the travaux préparatoires, but it must be the right thing to do to put the matter before a Board, who then decide the matter. As mentioned above, the Act does not give the parent or guardian the right to decide to terminate the pregnancy, only to submit the application for such. In addition to consideration by a Board, it is necessary to obtain the consent of the County Medical Officer (s.9(c)). Nor are there direct guidelines to help the County Medical Officer to reach a decision in cases subject to s.9. Since the mental status of the woman in itself comprises grounds for termination of pregnancy pursuant to s.2(3e), this must obviously be taken into account. This leads to much the same problem as in the case of women under the age of sixteen. The rules have not been considered in relation to each other.

There is even more reason to criticize the rules which apply to the group of women dealt with in this section than to criticize the rules applying to young and only slightly mentally retarded women, since the women referred to here are a group in special need of legal protection. Rules of procedure which protect a person from infringement of rights, and clear rules of responsibility, will be an important guarantee of legal security.

One of the first and least controversial exceptions to the prohibitions on termination of pregnancy refers especially to mentally retarded women and women suffering from severe mental illness. In the Abortion Act of 1960, one of the indications for termination of pregnancy was that the woman was "insane" or "had particularly impaired mental ability". This rule is perpetuated in the present Act, more or less unchanged. There has been some discussion of terms, and the term "insane" has been replaced by "suffering from severe mental illness" and the term "particularly impaired mental ability" by "mentally retarded to a considerable degree". The content of the term has thus been discussed and changed in line with medical developments, but the actual legal situation of these women has not been discussed. For women suffering from severe mental illness and women who are mentally retarded to a considerable degree, it is probably just as important to discuss their right to have children as their right to terminate pregnancy. This is a difficult question, but one which should not therefore "be swept under the carpet".

Termination of Pregnancy After the End of the Twelfth Week

The Main Principle: Abortion Decided by a Board

After the end of the twelfth week of pregnancy it is not the woman herself but a Board who decides whether an operation to terminate the pregnancy shall be performed or not (s.7(2)). Thus, in the case of women whose pregnancy has progressed to this stage, the old system of a Board and the principle of specific indications for termination of pregnancy have been maintained (s.2(3)), and the indications are the same as before the amendment to the Act in 1978.

There is no fixed time limit for how late in pregnancy a woman may apply to terminate the pregnancy, but the conditions for authorization of termination of pregnancy shall become more stringent as the duration of pregnancy increases (s.2(5)). After the end of the eighteenth week of pregnancy, termination of the pregnancy may be authorized in exceptional cases only – there must be "particularly important grounds for doing so" (s.2(6)). The most relevant grounds for terminating the pregnancy at such a late stage are hereditary ones, since it is difficult to assess the risk of hereditary defects before about the twentieth week of pregnancy (see Ot. prp. no. 53 (1977–78: 12). If there is reason to believe that the foetus is viable outside the womb, i.e. some time between the twenty-fourth and twenty-eighth weeks of pregnancy, it is no longer permitted to authorize termination of the pregnancy (s.2(6)). If the pregnancy does not develop normally after this time, it is regarded as ending in a stillbirth – not an abortion (possibly a premature birth).

The main reasons for these rules are ethical ones. It is assumed that all life – also the foetus – has a right to protection, but out of consideration for the woman this protection cannot be absolute. The right to legal protection increases with biological maturation, i.e. the duration of the pregnancy, and this is why rules have been established which gradually increase the legal protection of the foetus: self-determined termination of pregnancy during the first period of the pregnancy, followed by termination of pregnancy authorized by a Board, and finally, during the last stage of the pregnancy, a ban on induced abortion.

There is not only the ethical but also the medical aspect. The physical and mental strain will increase as the pregnancy progresses. At a later stage of the pregnancy, termination of the pregnancy requires a bigger operation, and an abortion is simplest and least risky when the operation can be performed at an early stage.

When the pregnancy is terminated during the first twelve weeks the risk of injury is minimal. The risk increases gradually with the duration of the pregnancy, but there are no clear limits – it is not decidedly more risky to terminate the pregnancy during the thirteenth than during the twelfth week (cf. St. meld. no. 17 (1982–83), section 4.3).

Thus, out of consideration for the woman herself, it is desirable to perform the operation as early as possible in the pregnancy. There is also another factor – termination of the pregnancy at a later stage requires more resources. On the other hand, a woman who applies for an abortion always has a reason – conscious or unconscious – for doing so, and this reason is often of a kind which makes it particularly unreasonable to reject her application. The short deadline for self-determined termination of pregnancy probably hits those with fewest resources hardest – those who have the greatest need to be granted an abortion.

However, it has been decided to maintain the system of Boards. The Primary Board consists of two doctors (s.7(2)). Section 21 stipulates the composition of the Board in more detail: one member shall be the medical superintendent of the unit where the operation is to be performed, the medical superintendent's deputy, or another doctor attached to the unit and chosen by the medical superintendent. In practice this will often mean the doctor at the unit who performs operations to terminate pregnancy. The other member of the Board is appointed by the County Medical Officer. This doctor shall have a knowledge of social medicine and shall not belong to the staff of the unit where the operation is to be performed. It is also specified that at least one of the two doctors should be a woman, but this is not an absolute requirement.

The Board of Appeal (cf. below concerning the course of procedure) is another Primary Board – that is to say, a Primary Board at another institution – supplemented by a third member (the Regulations s.22). This third member shall not be a doctor (medical practitioner) but a social worker or public health nurse with experience of social work. At least one of the members of the Appeals Board shall be a woman. The third member is appointed by the County Medical Officer.

Further Consideration of the Limits Between Self-determined Termination of Pregnancy, Termination Authorized by a Board, and the Probibition against Pregnancy Termination

As we have seen, the distinction between before and after the twelfth week of pregnancy is very important for a woman who wishes to terminate her pregnancy. Before this stage of the pregnancy she makes the decision herself, and only in exceptional cases can her decision be formally judicially reviewed. After this stage of pregnancy she has to apply to a Board. This is an extra strain on most women and, in at least thirty per cent of these cases the application is rejected (Weekly Statistical Report no. 12, 1982).

The decisive point in time is whether "it is possible to perform the operation before the twelfth week of pregnancy has elapsed" (the Abortion Act s.2(2)). In other words, there are two factors to be clarified; in the first place the duration of the pregnancy, and in the second place when it is possible to perform the operation. It is well known that it can be difficult to establish exactly how far a pregnancy has progressed – this is a matter of evaluation. According to page 40 of the Guidelines, the duration of pregnancy is calculated from the first day of the last menstrual period. Other supplementary information from the woman herself may also be relevant for this evaluation. Various methods of medical diagnostics can also be used, e.g. ultrasound diagnostics.

How quickly the operation can be performed will vary – usually it will not be possible for at least a couple of days. In other words, this will depend on the capacity at the institutions which have been approved for such operations (cf. s.3), and the distance from the institution. In any case, the time that elapses will vary from hospital to hospital. In other words, the Act means that women receive different treatment depending on where in the country they live. This, together with the fact that, in theory, the operation can be performed at once, supports the view that the Act should be understood to mean that, as long as the woman submits her application before the end of the twelfth week deadline, she has a right to decide herself – irrespective of whether the operation will, in fact, be carried out somewhat later.

Who is it then who has the final say in this matter which is so important to a woman? In the first instance it is the primary doctor who must take a standpoint on the matter, but it is the hospital doctor or the Board who has the final word: if the hospital doctor finds out that the primary doctor has assessed the case wrongly "the Board shall immediately refer the woman to a hospital unit or other institution where the operation may be performed" (s.7(1)). If the hospital doctor finds out that the Board or the primary doctor has assessed the case wrongly, he shall forward the application for termination of pregnancy to a Board (the Regulations s.5(5)). These rules tend to imply that the woman is not given the benefit of any doubt, irrespective of what the doubt is about. Section 7 assumes, in fact, that wrong assessments shall be righted without taking into account whether or not this is to the woman's advantage. It is "the right time" that is the important factor. However, there are strong grounds for not interpreting the rules too literally. The Ministry of Health and Social Affairs is also of the opinion that the matter should not be referred to a Board in cases of doubt (see page 25 of the Guidelines). The Act shall be interpreted literally only in cases where a serious error has been made when assessing the duration of pregnancy. It would be a terrible strain on a woman to be sent home from hospital with the message that she cannot have the operation at this stage after all – the case must first be submitted to a Board, and then "we shall see". In such cases it must be justifiable to protect the woman against a restricted interpretation of the law. This is because a liberal interpretation of the twelve-week time limit also argues that, even if there is increased risk connected to the operation, and the development of the foetus changes radically after the end of the twelfth week of pregnancy – these changes take place gradually.

The boundary between authorization of pregnancy termination by a Board and a ban on termination of pregnancy is by no means sharp. The same difficulties are encountered in determining duration of pregnancy. Furthermore, the rules are not based on fixed deadlines, but on the assumption that the conditions for authorization of termination of pregnancy shall become more stringent as duration of pregnancy increases (s.2(5) and (6)). After the eighteenth week of pregnancy has elapsed there must be particularly important grounds for terminating the pregnancy – one or more of the indications established in s.2(3) must apply very strongly. The prohibition against pregnancy termination is not connected to any specific point in time of the pregnancy, but to the time when the foetus is able to live independent of the woman. This is sometime between the twenty-fourth and twenty-eighth week of pregnancy, but no exact time has been specified. It is up to the Board to make a considered assessment of whether or not the woman's application should be granted. This is a free judgement where the duration of the pregnancy is only one of the factors to be taken into account. After the end of the twelfth week of pregnancy the woman does not have a right to an induced abortion – only the right to apply for one.

Handling of the Case by the Primary Board and the Appeals Board

The application for termination of pregnancy is submitted to a doctor also after the twelfth week of pregnancy has elapsed, but – if the woman so wishes – it can be submitted directly to a Board (s.5(1)). In this case the Primary Board takes on the functions of the primary doctor (the Regulations s.9).

Just as when the woman is less than thirteen weeks pregnant, the doctor shall examine her and assess the duration of the pregnancy (the Regulations s.8(1)). He/she shall similarly inform the woman about the nature of the operation and its medical consequences, and shall offer her advice on the services available and ethical counselling (s.5(2), s.2(1) and the Regulations s.8(2)).

Thus, instead of submitting the application directly to an institution, it is sent to a Board. The application shall be accompanied by a report on the observations made by the doctor, and the woman's reasons for applying for the operation (s.7). The woman may write the application herself, and state the reasons for it, or the doctor can do this in consultation with the woman. He has a duty to help her (ss.7(2) and 8 and the Regulations s.3). The doctor is also under obligation to act quickly (s.7).

The Board shall consider the case and make a decision as soon as possible (s.7).

The main source of information on which the Board bases its decision is the report from the primary doctor. In addition, the woman has a right to express an opinion to the Board, either verbally or in writing, and she has a right to attend the Board accompanied by another person (the Regulations s.11(3)). Major consideration shall be given to the woman's own assessment of her situation (s.2(4)). If the Board consider it necessary, and the woman gives her consent, they may also obtain information regarding the woman's situation from the health, social and insurance standpoints, notwithstanding the statutory obligation to observe professional secrecy (s.11). The Board is under obligation to inform the woman that she may refuse permission to obtain such information (the Regulations s.11(2)). Sections 4 and 9 also apply to termination after the end of the twelfth week of pregnancy. That is to say, it is necessary to obtain the opinion of the parent or guardian if the woman is under sixteen years of age or mentally retarded, and, if the woman is suffering from severe mental illness or is mentally retarded to a considerable degree, the application for termination of pregnancy may be submitted by the parent or guardian on her behalf.

The Board's decision shall be substantiated in writing as soon as it has been reached (s.8). Irrespective of the outcome, the woman, or possibly the parent or guardian, shall be informed as soon as possible. A woman's application for termination of pregnancy cannot be granted unless both members of the Board agree (the Regulations s.12(2)). If the application is approved, the reasons shall be stated with reference to the rules in the Act giving authorization for the approval. The woman shall also be informed of the date and place of admission to hospital.

If the application is rejected, the reasons shall include a brief account of the actual conditions which determined the decision. If considered necessary in order to enable the woman to understand the decision, she shall also be informed about the content of the legislation forming the basis for the decision. She shall also be told whether the decision was unanimous, and in cases of dissent both members shall state the reasons for their standpoint. In addition, the report shall also contain information on the woman's right to see the documents in the case, and about the system of appeal pursuant to s.8(2). If the woman does not withdraw the application for termination of pregnancy within three days after she has been notified of the rejection, the decision is examined by another Board. The woman may express a wish that the appeal be dealt with by a specific Board. According to the Regulations s.16, this wish should be complied with provided there are no strong reasons to the contrary. If she so wishes, the woman may provide the Appeals Board with supplementary information.

The case shall be dealt with by the Appeals Board according to the same rules as for the Primary Boards, and the decision shall be similarly substantiated.

A simple majority is sufficient for approval of an application by the Appeals Board (s.8(2)). In the event of dissent, and if it is the medical superintendent of the unit where the operation would normally be performed who is against the operation, the County Medical Officer shall ensure that the woman is transferred to another hospital unit where she can undergo the operation (the Regulations s.15). This procedure has been established out of consideration for the woman, who would otherwise have been treated by a doctor who disagreed with the approval of her application. In all probability, some doctors would also refuse to perform the operation.

If an application for termination of pregnancy is rejected by an Appeals Board this normally finally denies any further opportunity to have the pregnancy terminated legally. The woman can normally have her case considered anew by a Primary Board only at the request of the County Medical Officer, and only when there is fresh information available (the Regulations s.17).

The Indications

We must ask then, on what grounds does a woman have the right to termination of pregnancy after the end of the twelfth week?

According to s.2(3a), the pregnancy may be terminated for *reasons of health*, when "the pregnancy, childbirth or care of the child may result in unreasonable strain on the physical or mental health of the woman". It is important to note that it is not only the actual pregnancy and childbirth that are relevant for this assessment, but also care of the child. Similarly that any mental strain is just as important as physical strain. The term "unreasonable strain" must either imply a greater strain than is normal during pregnancy, childbirth and care of the child, or that the strain is unreasonable seen in relation to the woman's mental and physical resources (cf. Guidelines: 27). It is further stated that the law shall take into account whether the woman has "any predisposition to illness". This does not mean that the woman must be especially predisposed to illness in order to be granted termination of pregnancy for health reasons, but if she is so disposed, this will make it easier for her to obtain approval of her application.

According to s.2(3b), a woman may be granted termination of pregnancy for *social reasons*, if "the pregnancy, childbirth or care of the child may place the woman in a difficult life situation". This indication is the one which most often gives the woman the right to terminate the pregnancy, alone or combined with the indication of reasons of health. The difficult situation must not be temporary, nor capable of being counteracted by ordinary measures of social welfare. Some typical factors which may be relevant are listed on page 27 et seq. of the Guidelines. The first factor is the woman's age. It may often be especially difficult for a young woman to have a child. This might obstruct her education, and decide her life to an extreme degree. Responsibility for her own life may be difficult enough: responsibility for a child as well could easily be an unreasonable burden. The practical requirements will often be totally lacking. If the woman is fairly old it may also be a strain to have a child. In the case of these women the health and social reasons will often be synergistic.

Another factor is whether the woman is responsible for children already. Responsibility for yet another child may be "the straw that breaks the camel's back".

Also important are the woman's family conditions in the broadest sense of the term. The woman may have very much to cope with already, or she may be met with prejudice and rejection. Another very important factor is the woman's relationship with the father; can she expect him to support her, or does she have no contact with him at all?

The last factor to be mentioned is the nature of her other living conditions – her situation as regards a place to live, education and work. If the child will lead to greater problems than normal, this would appear to argue in favour of approval of the application. The assessment of the application shall take into account the woman's own physical and mental resources.

According to s.2(3c), a third indication justifying termination of pregnancy is *hereditary reasons*, i.e. if "there is a major risk that the child may suffer from a serious risk as a result of its genotype, or disease or harmful influences during pregnancy". The term "major risk" implies that there must be a more than a normal risk that the child may come to suffer from a serious disease. No limit has been established for the size of this risk. It must be assessed in each case, and must be considered in relation to the woman's life situation (ibid: 29 et seq.). The term serious disease refers both to physical and mental diseases and injuries.

According to s.2(4), when assessing whether one or more of the above indications exist for termination of pregnancy, the Board shall take into account the woman's overall situation. This assumes a concrete and individual assessment. The same provision requires the Board to give major consideration to the woman's own assessment of her situation.

The fourth indication for termination of pregnancy can simply be called *ethical reasons*. These reasons are listed in s.2(3d). They can again be divided into two groups. In the first group, pregnancy due to violation of sexual consent, or more precisely if the woman has become pregnant under the conditions referred to in ss.192–199 of the Penal Code. These provisions stipulate punishment for, *inter alia*, rape, and for sexual intercourse with minors. The second group includes pregnancy due to so-called incest. Pursuant to the Penal Code, sexual intercourse with close relatives (defined in the Code) is a punishable offence.

It is not a condition that the woman reports the crime to the police. Therefore it is up to the Board to judge whether the pregnancy is due to such conditions. No guidelines have been laid down as to the extent to which the crime must be proved.

If the Board concludes that the pregnancy is due to a punishable offence of the kind referred to above, it is not the intention that they assess whether the woman has good enough grounds to terminate pregnancy in her situation – s.2(4) does not apply to s.2(3d). Such crimes are regarded as so serious that there is no right to force the woman to complete the pregnancy to term. Nevertheless, after the end of the eighteenth week of pregnancy, it is assumed that the Board assesses the reasons in more detail, since the rule stating that there must be particularly important grounds for terminating a pregnancy after the eighteenth week has elapsed applies to all induced abortions.

However, in the light of the above, we can ask whether all women under the age of sixteen years do, in fact, have a right to termination of pregnancy before the end of the eighteenth week of the pregnancy. If a women under the age of sixteen is pregnant she has obviously had sexual intercourse and, pursuant to ss.196–197 of the Penal Code it is a punishable offence to have sexual intercourse with a person under the age of 16 years. If the man is of "about the same age and maturity" (ss.195(4) and 196(3)) the punishment may not actually be applied, but the Abortion Act s.2(3d) employs the term "as a result of circumstances covered by ss.192–199 of the Penal Code". This issue is not raised in the travaux préparatoires or in the Guidelines. The fact of the matter is that, in the Guidelines, there is no mention at all of ss.195–196 (ibid: 30 et seq.).

There are strong reasons for stating that all persons under the age of sixteen years should have a right to terminate a pregnancy also after the end of the twelfth week. It would be very unfortunate to force someone to become a mother at so young an age, and this is possibly a major reason why young age in itself has been made an indication for termination of pregnancy. Given such an interpretation, the consideration by a Board of applications for termination of pregnancy from girls under the age of sixteen years becomes a formality, and could therefore be done away with. There is no way to do this, however, with the law as it stands today.

The fifth and last indication for termination of pregnancy is if the woman is *suffering from severe mental illness* (s.2(3e)). The Act uses the terms "severe mental illness" and "mentally retarded to a considerable degree", and these terms must be interpreted in the same way as in s.4. In the case of this indication too, it is not the intention that the Board evaluate whether the woman concerned has sufficient grounds to terminate the pregnancy. Section 2(4) does not apply to s.2(3e). The same question then arises as in the case of s.2(3d). In addition it is often the case that the woman herself has not applied for termination of the pregnancy. Her parent or guardian has done so. The solution should not depend on whether the pregnancy is of less or more than twelve weeks duration. Therefore, a reasonable interpretation of s.2(3) would be that the duration of the pregnancy should not be considered of any importance in the case of applications from women suffering from severe mental illness or who are mentally retarded to a considerable degree, at any rate not before the duration of the pregnancy has exceeded eighteen weeks.

Notes

* This article was first published in Tove Stang Dahl (ed.), *Kvinnerett II*. Oslo: Universitetsforlaget, 1985.

1 This chapter is based mainly on information from "Abortlovgivningens historie" (History of abortion legislation) by Brita H. Gulli in the book *Det kriminelle kjønn* (The Criminal Sex).

5

What Kind of Children? A New Content to the Debate on Abortion*

HENRIETTE SINDING AASEN

Introduction and Approach to the Problem

To a large degree, the debate on induced abortion has been concerned with who should have the legal authority to decide in individual cases – the woman or a public agency. The *ethical foundation* for decisions to terminate pregnancy is another topic altogether. In this connection two particular conditions have been discussed: The right to destroy life in general, and social conditions as a basis for termination of pregnancy. Advances in *prenatal diagnosis*, which have made it easier to obtain definitive information about the foetus, have drawn increasing attention to the grounds for decisions to terminate pregnancy. What kind of information on the *foetus* should influence the choice of whether or not to have an abortion? Many people are critical towards the possibility of a larger number of selective abortions – operations to terminate pregnancy because of demonstrated conditions or properties of the foetus. It is asserted, for example, that selective abortions violate the principle that all human beings are of equal worth, irrespective of their properties. This is a totally different problem from those connected to the large number of "blind" terminations of pregnancy (operations that are carried out for reasons other than the condition of the foetus).

The intention of this chapter is to contribute to the discussion about prenatal diagnosis and selective termination of pregnancy. I find it necessary to emphasize that any study of problems of a fundamental ethical nature will always be influenced by personal scales of values. It is difficult to be fair to other ways of thinking, even if these belong within the framework of a more holistic understanding of the problem. For this reason I hope that the picture presented here will be filled out by others with perhaps a different viewpoint.

My scale of values is rooted in the conception that all human beings are of equal worth, irrespective of intellectual and physical abilities, sex and other properties. My views are not founded on religion, but are inspired by current humanistic thinking – which in turn has absorbed many of the values of Christianity.

The main theme of this chapter is the development of real possibilities of selection – and the importance of this situation for society's view of humanity and the autonomy of the individual.

Prenatal Diagnosis

Prenatal diagnosis includes various medical investigations of the foetus. The purpose of the investigations is to chart the health of the foetus, which includes discovering possible chromosome defects, monogenic hereditary diseases and structural deformities (Bjøro 1987). The Ministry of Health and Social Affairs has stated that: ". . . the purpose should be to arrange for such prenatal diagnosis in all cases where there is known to be increased risk of genetic/congenital defects in the offspring. Down's syndrome is still important in connection with this type of diagnosis" (St. meld. no. 73 (1981–82): 15).

In Norway pregnant women who will have reached the age of thirty-eight years by the time they give birth are offered amniocentesis during the fifteenth to seventeenth week of pregnancy. Because one per cent of women in the age group thirty-seven to thirty-eight years and about two per cent in the age group forty years risk giving birth to children with chromosome defects, these women are regarded as belonging to a risk group (St. meld. no. 73 (1981–82): 22). Amniocentesis is also offered to women who have previously given birth to a child with a chromosome defect or a defect of the neural tube (e.g. spinal hernia), or if there is reason to suspect a serious hereditary disease.

The ultrasound examination – offered to all pregnant women in Norway once or twice during pregnancy – is becoming an effective technique for discovering Down's syndrome in the foetus (Salvesen et al. 1990: 701–704). Ultrasound can also demonstrate serious malformations of the foetus. The development of this form of diagnosis also enables discovery of less serious physical abnormalities.

A test of the placenta in the eighth to tenth week of pregnancy enables early diagnosis of chromosome abnormalities and defects of the neural tube. Serum-alpha-protein investigations, which measure the concentration of protein in the amniotic fluid, can help to bring to light open neural tubes and chromosome defects. In addition, the development of DNA technology provides a general possibility of early and conclusive diagnosis of genetically determined conditions. In future, a test of the mother's blood will be able to provide new possibilities of prenatal diagnosis without operation (Bjøro 1987: 119), and can already confirm the sex of the foetus. The rest of this chapter does not focus on the ethical implications of obtaining information about the sex of the foetus.

Even when investigations of the foetus indicate that something is wrong, some of the techniques do not always provide one hundred per cent reliable information. We know of foetuses that have been removed on inadequate grounds. However, the development of new techniques seems to provide increasingly more reliable information and, in order to improve the reliability, different methods of investigation can be combined. For example, amniocentesis or a foetal blood test can be performed when the ultrasound examination leads one to suspect Down's syndrome (Salvesen et al. 1990: 703).

The Framework of the Abortion Act

Section 2(2) of the Abortion Act provides the authority for self-determined termination of pregnancy up to the end of the twelfth week. This implies that up to that time, a woman has a legal right to have her pregnancy terminated, and she is not required to state her reasons for doing so. Section 2(3c) implies that an abortion may be granted after the end of the twelfth week of pregnancy if "there is a major risk that the child may suffer from a serious disease as a result of its genotype, or disease or harmful influences during pregnancy". This provision is the one which currently provides authorization for the majority of induced abortions because of confirmed disease or developmental defects in the foetus. Because the pregnancy has progressed to a stage where consideration for the woman has to be weighed against consideration for the foetus and general ethical considerations, the decision has to be made by an Abortion Board. However, the conditions that are most often confirmed by prenatal diagnosis are assumed to be within the ambit of the Act (Down's syndrome, and defect development of the brain and spinal cord).

When the pregnancy has lasted for more than twelve weeks the Act requires major risk of *serious* disease. From 0–12 weeks, during which period the woman has the right to decide herself, there is no requirement regarding degree of seriousness. The Abortion Act is ambiguous in this respect. If during this period of twelve weeks the woman gets herself tested by various techniques of prenatal diagnosis, and these bring to light less serious conditions in the foetus, it is impossible, given today's Abortion Act, to prevent her from having the pregnancy terminated. The further discussions assume that the Abortion Act remains unchanged.

More about the Approach to the Problem

In earlier days, having no possibility to "check" the offspring was part of the mystery of life. Today's advances in prenatal diagnosis imply that the choices involved in reproduction will to a greater degree include taking a qualitative standpoint on the foetus: even if I essentially want children, do I – if I can avoid it – want a handicapped child or a child that is "different"?

The question becomes particularly relevant in the light of better possibilities of *early* diagnosis – before the end of the twelfth week of pregnancy. This is because the right of self-determination makes this approach to the problem the "common property" of all women. In my view, whether the information on the foetus is obtained before or after the end of the twelfth week of pregnancy does not change the ethical aspects of the situation. It is probable, however, that early information on the foetus will lead to a larger number of selective abortions and thus *make these more general.* At the same time, there is a trend in the direction of more *detailed* diagnosis. It will be possible not only to demonstrate serious functional disabilities or diseases but also conditions which cannot easily be described as serious (for example, hare lip or cleft plate). This is another aspect which leads to generalization of a qualitative assessment of human life.

The discussion about what kind of information on the foetus should influence the choice to terminate pregnancy, and the discussion about who should be responsible for a possible decision to terminate a pregnancy in the light of the available information – the woman or a public agency – must be kept completely separate. Essentially, the material discussion and the discussion of "personnel", although tending to overlap, involve different considerations. If the question of *who* should make the decision is made the primary issue, this implies that the material discussion on the ethical and social aspects connected to "quality control" of the foetus is pushed into the background.

Is It Wrong to Have Better Opportunities to Choose? – Introduction

Is it wrong for a mother or a couple to be able to *choose* to terminate a pregnancy if prenatal diagnosis shows that the child will be abnormal? Seen from the standpoint of the individual, it is neither unnatural nor indecent to *want* a healthy and perfectly developed child. An essential question, however, is whether the transition from wishing to actually having the opportunity to choose does not become a problem in a larger perspective.

In the extreme, prenatal diagnosis can be regarded as a purely medical concern; the purpose of the diagnosis is to investigate the state of health of the child. Moreover, it is doctors who inform the woman about prenatal diagnosis, tell her the results of the investigation, and discuss what conclusions can be drawn from the result. However, "The medical basis can hide the fact that prenatal diagnosis – in a totally different way from diagnosis of disease – gives actuality to fundamental ethical issues. This is a question of our view of humanity, our values, and what principles should direct our actions. It finally concerns the psychological, social and moral consequences of choosing the one or the other course of action" (SOU 1989: 74).

The development and use of prenatal diagnosis should have given rise to the following question at a far earlier stage: how will real possibilities of subjecting the foetus to "quality control" influence society's view of humanity? Recently, however, several critical voices have been heard, especially from Christian and humanistic circles. It is almost too late; rapid advances mean that the methods for early and detailed diagnosis are being taken into use at a fast pace, while there seems to be little will for a thorough debate of the issues.

Because of the new information it provides, the use of prenatal diagnosis seems to give women and couples new opportunities to choose. Another problem to be studied is whether or not this gives them more autonomy.

The Fundamental Principle of the Equal Worth of All Human Beings

The term "human worth" is difficult to define precisely, though it can be expressed in many ways. One way of expressing the principle is to say that all people are of equal worth, or quality. "Worth" does not refer to any tangible standard of measurement. The idea is rather that a person's worth is something that cannot be measured or weighed; as human beings we are all equal, independent of properties and functional abilities.

What could be the effect on human worth if diseased and functionally handicapped foetuses can be removed *because of* this condition?

> There is probably an important ethical distinction between a situation where a pregnancy is terminated because one does not want to have a child and a situation where it is terminated because one is told that the awaited child is defective. In the later case it is the principle of the equal worth of all human beings, irrespective of handicaps or other differences, that is threatened (SOU 1989: 83).

This quotation expresses the ethical difference between "blind" and selective abortions, which is that selective abortions threaten the principle of the equal worth of all human beings, irrespective of properties. In the following pages I discuss the application of this principle at an individual level and from the point of view of society.

In a concrete situation of choice, where a woman decides to have an operation to remove an abnormal foetus, her choice is not necessarily a consequence of disdain for sick or handicapped people. She usually has other reasons for terminating the pregnancy. A common motive is that she cannot cope with caring for a child who will demand much more of her and the family than a normal, healthy child would. It is her own needs and her family's needs that argue for terminating the pregnancy, not their view of sick or handicapped people. Therefore it cannot be generally maintained that an abortion because of a demonstrated defect in the foetus expresses that the people concerned have little respect for sick and handicapped people.

Seen "from within", each individual chooses as she feels she must in a given situation. Often the woman and/or the family apply a form of *jus necessitatis*, where their own situation is weighed against the child's possibility of living a life of quality, taking into account what they know about the condition, and keeping in mind the everyday life that they can offer. However, even if the individual persons do not intend to violate the principle of the equal worth of all human beings, this may in fact be the case. Seen "from without", the principle is violated because a distinction is made between a sick and a healthy foetus. In the light of this fact I assume that the individual's choice and actions must be studied in a broader social perspective, where the choices made by individuals reflect the surrounding social "climate". This assumption will be discussed in more detail below.

If the problem is placed in this broader perspective, the focus is turned away from the personal dilemma of the woman and her family. Attention is drawn instead to social structures and social expressions of how people are expected to adjust to society. This contributes to a better understanding of the fundamental view of humanity which characterizes the organization of society. This also makes it possible to study what violates general expectations concerning a person as a participant in society. The term human worth must also have a place in this complex.

View of Humanity – Human Worth

A socially oriented perspective draws attention to structures and not to individuals. What signal does the use of methods to discover abnormalities of the foetus in the mother's womb convey about society's view of humanity and choice of values?

Prenatal Diagnosis as Society's "Solution"?

Is there a causal relationship between the use of prenatal diagnosis and the unsatisfactory help and support for handicapped persons in society? The answer is not immediately clear. In a future perspective it is totally realistic for society both to improve conditions for the various groups of handicapped persons, and simultaneously to decide to offer prenatal diagnosis to women at high risk of giving birth to handicapped children, or possibly to all women. On the other hand, considering how society *currently* deals with its responsibility to care for people with special needs, it is obvious that there is a long way to go before the organization of society takes into account the fact that not all people have the same abilities, either physical or mental. In my opinion this is *one* of the reasons for the development and use of prenatal diagnosis, naturally combined with other factors, such as the interests of the scientists themselves.

By offering prenatal diagnosis society makes it possible for a woman to undergo an operation to remove an abnormal foetus. This signals certain attitudes; for example, that handicapped children are a burden for which the individual family cannot always be expected to accept responsibility. Sympathy is expressed for people who give birth to children who are different. Since the parents of handicapped children often do have more responsibility than other parents, this sympathy is in fact deserved. It is placed in a somewhat pecular light, however, when it does not make society try to provide satisfactory conditions for handicapped persons and their providers.

In St. meld. no. 73 (1981–82), the Ministry of Health and Social Affairs states that the assessment of the degree to which prenatal diagnostic services should be extended is not based on so-called "costs-benefit" analysis (see e.g. pp. 14 and 16). The only relevant issue is consideration for the families concerned. On the other hand, economic calculations are included openly in the debate in other countries. In an English publication it is stated that an economic calculation of the use of prenatal diagnosis and genetic counselling "generally indicates that it actually saves money, in the sense that it averts cost increases which would otherwise be inevitable . . . it is cheaper to screen and counsel the whole population than it is to treat affected children who would otherwise be born to unprepared couples" (Royal College of Physicians of London 1989: 40).

To what degree does society signal that prenatal diagnosis is a "solution" to the problems which handicapped persons represent for their surroundings? If the declining will to adapt conditions in society to meet different needs is combined with more widespread use of methods to discover abnormal foetuses, then this must be regarded as society's solution. It can also be regarded as a material approach to human life: society establishes the rule that only those who meet the demand to "conform with the contract" are truly welcome members of society. Those who exhibit "non-conformities" are only partly welcome; it is up to the individual family to decide whether they wish to accept the child – this is considered to be a private matter. A "different" child is not always regarded as belonging to human existence, but one which we, as controlling individuals, can accept or reject.

Industrial society encourages the growth of a view of humanity which implies that: "we are born by chance, live a life determined by internal and external circumstances, and die . . . The obvious consequence of this all too narrow picture of human life is that all handicapped persons are only a kind of misunderstanding, and to society are expensive and irrational deviations from the normal and successful" (Parmann 1989).

A human being thus becomes more a "product" than a life with a right to unconditional respect; a human being becomes more an object than a subject. An argument against this interpretation is that the use of prenatal diagnosis on the one hand and society's care for the handicapped on the other do not exclude each other. Neither in theory nor in practice is there anything to prevent society from investing resources in both. Some persons will maintain that if there were to be fewer handicapped persons, conditions would be better for all of them because there would be more resources available for each of them. It is my opinion that society's lack of effort for the sick and the handicapped – persons that are "different" – is one of the *reasons* for the use, and "need", of prenatal diagnosis.

Should Human Worth Be a Function of Way of Life?

> Considerable emphasis is placed on people's ability to produce and consume. "Consume" does not only refer to food and drink, but also art and culture, theatre, films, books, pictures, sport and music, exercise and singsongs. All these have increasingly become consumer goods, and each individual is assessed by his or her ability to produce or consume these goods. The decisive factor becomes how the person functions as producer and consumer. This leads to a functionalistic view of humanity (Church Council Working Group 1989: 38).

This quotation describes how society's expectations concerning people's way of life influence its view of humanity: people are evaluated according to their capacity for production and consumption.

It is often more difficult for handicapped persons than for others to produce and consume these goods, and for this reason they do not conform to the conception of a "successful" way of life. This description is incomplete, however, since it does not take into account that the handicapped can also produce and consume goods, even if they do this in a different way and the goods have a different content. Nils Christie describes how, in country villages, the "extraordinary people" (he chooses this term in preference to "mentally handicapped") are involved in culture and intellectual activities:

> In these very villages where so many people can neither read nor write a large number are intellectually inclined. Wherever one goes, and whatever the time of day, there are study circles, seminars, courses and lectures in progress . . . Through living in

> these villages, and also when I visit them, I am struck again and again by the fact that here, in these places, I find myself more among intellectuals than in the university with which I am familiar (Christie 1989: 67).

Christie questions whether ordinary society can offer "extraordinary" people a good enough life over and above material things, "measured by criteria such as diversity of social and cultural participation" (Christie 1989: preface). He is particularly concerned with the need for human contact with, and stimulation from, others who are more like themselves than so-called "normal" people. His respect for the "extraordinary" is the reason for his scepticism towards integrating these people into ordinary society. It is simultaneously an expression of the fact that ordinary society in general is not adjusted to the needs of people who are different, so that they easily become clients on the premisses of the prevailing system, instead of people on their own premisses.

People who do not "conform to pattern" often do not have an opportunity to live a life in accordance with their own abilities, because society is not arranged to meet special needs. Society does not give them sufficient alternatives to fulfil their right to live a worthy life – a life of quality, on their own premisses – or their right to realize their own potentials.

Use of prenatal diagnosis for the purpose of giving women the possibility of choosing an abortion supports the view that certain people should preferably not have been born, out of consideration for themselves or out of consideration for their surroundings. This again confirms society's expectations regarding people whose lives and experiences "conform to pattern". We are almost told that people who do not conform to ordinary ways of life do not fit well into our society. This may make us less and less capable of accepting people on their own premisses. Human worth will become more closely linked to the ability to function in society.

To Sum Up

It seems that the distinction between people and manipulable objects is gradually becoming diffuse, and that the functionalistic view of humanity is helping to consolidate human worth as a function of the ability to produce and consume in a "normal" and widest sense of the term. Instead of arranging society to make it easier to live as an "extraordinary" person, methods are being introduced which imply that an increasing number of "problem" persons are never born. This means that we can glimpse the contours of a more and more streamlined and inflexible society.

Personal Autonomy – The Question of Giving Women Better Opportunities to Choose

A weighty argument put forward in favour of prenatal diagnosis is that it gives each woman or couple an opportunity to *choose* – to decide in advance – whether or not to have an abnormal child (St. meld. no. 73 (1981–82): 15). The Ministry does not regard it as unethical that prenatal diagnosis gives women an opportunity to terminate a pregnancy which would result in a handicapped child. On the contrary, it is asserted as highly ethical to give individuals a greater degree of self-determination in the form of better opportunities to make an informed choice. It is assumed that this strengthens the autonomy of the individual. This was also the reason put forward by professionals for introducing and using prenatal diagnosis.

In situations where a woman has the legal right to terminate her pregnancy – either because the pregnancy has not come further than twelve weeks, or because other conditions stipulated in the Abortion Act are fulfilled – the woman still has to make a choice. She will naturally receive impulses from her surroundings, and this external context strongly influences her choice. In the following section I discuss some of the elements of this context, and consider the relationship between context and the autonomy of the individual.

Why Do Women Want Prenatal Diagnosis?

It is not unusual for pregnant women to be worried that something may be wrong with the foetus. This anxiety is one of the reasons for the demand for prenatal diagnosis, since it touches upon the very core of the need for the services. New technology probably does not help to reduce this anxiety, quite the opposite (Leuzinger & Rambert 1988: 244). The increasing number of tests that "must" be used only serves to stimulate the anxiety. On the other hand, the anxiety of some women is reduced by confirmation that the foetus is not suffering from a particular condition. This may get the women to complete a pregnancy which they would otherwise have terminated. Prenatal diagnosis can never give a guarantee, however, that the foetus has no "defects".

Why are women afraid to give birth to a sick or handicapped child? One reason is knowing what it costs to care for such a child in today's society. Standing alone in the fight to give the child a worthy life – a life of quality – in a society that is unprepared to receive it is not an attractive prospect for the future. These are very general assumptions and refer most of all to the most serious forms of handicaps.

Social norms are negative towards handicap and regard the birth of a child with a handicap as a tragedy (Kaufmann 1988: 133). This again helps to increase the fear of giving birth to a child that is different.

Very little is said about the *positive* experience that often results from having a handicapped child in the family. Dr. Irmgard Nittert (1988) interviewed about a hundred parents where the mother had unexpectedly given birth to a handicapped child or a child that was different. Her investigation shows that the family's experiences were often positive. The fact that so little is said about the positive aspects may mean that, in a situation of choice, the mother or couple is not fully informed, and the decision is taken on a shaky foundation.

Another reason for wanting prenatal diagnosis may be fear of feeling that the woman is to blame for the awaited child's disease or handicap – that it was her fault. All women are offered an ultrasound examination and, according to the midwife Inger Eide, almost none refuse this offer (The hearing "Quality of life before life?" 27.9.89). As she understood it, the women were afraid of subsequent feelings of guilt if anything was shown to be wrong with the child.

In another study Tjeerd Tymstra has shown that the motivation was often to remove uncertainty:

> From our survey it appeared that the expectant mothers did not so much undergo the ultrasound to prevent having an abnormal child, but instead used the diagnostic procedure as a means of "losing their uncertainty" ... However, some of the women indicated that they had the feeling that the procedures were rather forced on them. ("It was for my own security," they said, "but I didn't feel at all insecure"; "I am having the test because everybody seems to want me to") (Tymstra 1989: 209).

These quotations are also an expression of the external pressure on the woman, and how *her own* experience of security can be threatened by an offer of "security". They also show that the woman is made an amateur in her own pregnancy, since the technological experts take over more and more in the form of supervisors. Tymstra also refers to a study of thirty women who had received a letter offering them a serum-alpha-photoprotein investigation:

> It appeared that some of the women had more or less consciously cut themselves off from the information offered to them ("I am somewhat wary of this sort of thing, I'd rather not think about it") or had put the information folder away ("I immediately hid it away in a drawer and forgot about it"). Some of the expectant mothers were visibly worried when we reminded them of the diagnostic test. But others clearly had the feeling that they should heed the possibility. ("Imagine if it turns out that there is something wrong with the baby later on") (ibid: 209).

It is not absolutely clear what these statements mean, and they must be interpreted in the context in which they are presented. Nevertheless, each of them expresses in its own way that the woman is confronted with a future reality which she is not sure that she wants to look into.

Tymstra's studies lead her to conclude that many women obviously find it difficult to refuse an offer of prenatal diagnosis (ibid: 209).

Based on a study of 211 women, Berit Sjøgren and Nils Uddenberg show that: "although they felt free about whether to undergo PND [prenatal diagnosis] or not, [they] considered it difficult to refrain from PND when it was offered. This is contradictory and might reflect that the autonomy is limited" (Sjøgren & Uddenberg 1988: 271).

If a woman refuses prenatal diagnosis and later gives birth to an abnormal child, this is no longer, as before, a matter of fate. The situation is rather that the woman may feel, and may be regarded by others, as responsible.

Sjøgren & Uddenberg interpret the results of their study as follows:

> . . . some women might have experienced pressure from society to produce a perfect baby. They might have felt that society, by providing the opportunity to PND, demands a loyalty that includes a duty to utilize the diagnostic method, and by aborting a defective fetus save the society the responsibility of a disabled child. Thus, many women – in spite of formal voluntariness – feel an obligation to have the fetus investigated (ibid: 271).

The studies referred to above indicate that the arguments stating that prenatal diagnosis gives the woman more autonomy do not agree with the situation as experienced by many women themselves.

The Relation Between Context and Choosing Abortion

Do women feel pressurized from outside into choosing abortion if the investigation shows that something is wrong? Even if the woman is not directly encouraged to terminate the pregnancy, she may nevertheless feel that she has little choice. Her choice is not made in a vacuum, but in a society with values and medical services which signal that it is the right thing to do to remove a handicapped foetus by abortion. What kind of "choice" is made in such a context? Is this not rather a question of "directing" individual persons, rather than an offer of choice? Furthermore: "'The Welfare State' is diminishing, so that the public sector as a whole has less resources available for care and services . . .. Is there then anything to justify real freedom of choice under such premisses?" (Nordborg 1987: 88).

The question is whether both freedom and choice are not directed by a technological imperative and the attitudes this creates, and whether, in reality, this is not a form of coercion, masked as a liberalistic "freedom" which does not take into account the premisses for the freedom of choice: one chooses as one *has to*, under the prevailing conditions: "Until mechanisms exist that give the public a decisive choice in setting the scientific and technical agenda, and until scientists and physicians are made more accountable to the people whose lives they change, technical innovations do not constitute new choices. They merely replace previous social constraints with new ones" (Hubbard 1986: 241).

Mass screening of women in order to discover specific diseases would further reduce the freedom of choice. It becomes even more difficult to refuse the investigation, and the subsequent choice to terminate the pregnancy must be seen in this context. Society has already made a choice: these diseases are such a burden that it is best that no one be born with them. The traditional legal concept of voluntariness is based on the right of informed consent. In this case this concept is inadequate, because the consent and the voluntariness are obstructed by society's "manifesto" concerning prevention of the birth of people with such diseases.

In my opinion, the arguments which emphasize greater autonomy for the woman do not give adequate consideration to the fact that she makes her choice in a social context. They ignore the fact that the offers in themselves may exert a pressure which reduces her freedom and extent of self-determination. They also ignore the fact that the offers imply management of individuals at the expense of the desired self-determination.

Conclusions and Challenges

Consideration for the woman's autonomy is ambiguous, and is therefore not a strong argument for prenatal diagnosis. On the basis of values, I am not a supporter of a development where a qualitative assessment of the foetus becomes an integrated part of the choice made by the individual concerning an abortion. This view is founded on the regard for preserving respect for human worth. In my opinion, the use of prenatal diagnosis as motivation for an abortion threatens to undermine the principle of the equal worth of all human beings, irrespective of their properties.

Since society in principle supports the view that human worth cannot be graded according to physical and mental ability, this should be reflected to a greater degree than at present in the actual shaping of society. Society must accept a clearer obligation to provide opportunities for everyone to realize their own potentials in life. This would provide a better starting point for a life of good quality, also for people who are "different".

Notes

* This article was first published in Retfærd, *Nordisk juridisk tidsskrift* (Nordic Legal Journal), No. 50, 1990.

6

Legal Regulation of New Reproductive Technologies: Continuity and Interconnectedness versus Freedom and Justice*

ANNE HELLUM

Women's Bodies, Reproductive Change, Values and the Law

To cure infertility, discover congenital disorders of the foetus or to treat the foetus by surgery is in this chapter seen as but one of the aspects of new reproductive technologies, ranging from *in vitro* fertilization, prenatal diagnosis to perinatal medicine.

This chapter is mainly concerned with the interplay between new reproductive technologies and legal and moral values linked to women's bodies and reproductive capacity.

Until recently human reproduction, both physically and conceptually, was tied to the woman's body. The process of ovulation, conception, gestation and birth took place inside and was a part of the woman's body. The process of life was mediated through the woman and her experiences. Law and religion in western societies mirror this. Roman law saw the foetus as a part of the female body. In catholic belief the woman has a special position as the guardian of the mysteries of life.

New reproductive technologies such as *in vitro* fertilization, egg donation, embryo donation, prenatal diagnosis and foetal medicine have both physically and conceptually separated the reproductive process from the woman's body. Conception is externalized and separated from the woman's body by *in vitro* fertilization. Egg donation and embryo donation has created a dividing line between the woman's uterus and the egg. External management and control of pregnancy is made possible by prenatal tests and foetal medicine. Medically the foetus is seen as a person separate from the mother.

Human reproduction may now partially be separated from the private, bodily, sexual and human sphere and integrated in the public, medical, professional or commercial sphere. Reproductive relations may thus become professionalized or commercialized. These changes in reproductive relations and conditions and in perceptions of maternity and the maternal/foetal relation may be understood as a process of change from an internal to an external mode of human reproduction.

The situation resembles the industrial revolution in Europe at the turn of the century. Just as the industrial revolution's machines, factories and accumulation of capital split up the family as a productive unit, the revolution within medical technology today may split up the heterosexual couple and the female body as reproductive units.

In the moral critique of new reproductive technologies, Christian ethical traditions have focused on the undermining of the institution of marriage and the nuclear family, while feminists' main concern has been the separation of the body from the process of reproduction.

The detachment of conception from the body, the division between uterus and egg and between mother and foetus, has given legislation a crucial place in this part of the process of human reproduction. Externalization makes direct management, control and manipulation with motherhood possible. The reproductive order which formerly was mainly regulated by the woman's body has been disturbed by the new combinations of egg, semen and uterus offered by new reproductive technologies. A moral and legal chaos has been created.

The technological and medical possibilities represent powerful, ethical, moral, political and legal challenges. The practice of new reproductive technology has been addressed by ethical and legal committees in Australia, the United States, Latin America, Europe and Asia. In this ongoing process of technological, moral and legal change, economic, professional, public and gender interests are involved.

A fundamental criticism which may be raised against most official ethical and legal recommendations is the gender neutral approach:

- Women's bodies and reproductive capacity are most directly involved by the development of new reproductive technologies. Women are the actual users or targets of these technologies, as involuntarily childless or as pregnant mothers.
- New reproductive technologies do not only affect women who are directly involved by taking up the actual medical and technological services which are offered. Indirectly, the technological

development affects all women by influencing the perception of and underlying values of women's bodies, reproductive capacities and maternity. The limits set by the woman's body are now in the process of being replaced by medical procedures and statutory regulation. Today the interplay between law and technology affects values that have been attached to the process of conception, pregnancy and birth.

- Research in women's law has revealed that women's position in law and society is closely linked to the society's ideas and values concerning women's bodies and reproductive capacities. In Norway birth law has emerged as a central discipline within women's law (Fastvold 1977, 1985a; Dahl 1987). Within birth law various ethical, cultural, social, medical and legal aspects of the reproductive process as experienced by women are systematized, interpreted and discussed.

In order to assess the technological and legal development, women-centred policy considerations may be useful analytical tools. Women-centred policy considerations may also serve as guidelines for future regulation of new reproductive technologies. The interests and values of individual childless women and women as a group ought to be identified and discussed.

On the one hand, feminist philosophical, ethical and political trends adapting a holistic, materialistic and dialectic approach towards conception, pregnancy and birth concerned with maternity as a central basis of human values have developed an understanding which leads to great emphasis being placed on considerations such as continuity and interconnectedness. This view is linked to an outlook on maternity as internal, continuous and interconnected. In legal politics it is claimed that the access to technology ought to be restricted by legislation in order to maintain basic human values.

On the other hand, the claim of reproductive freedom of individual women anchored in liberal theory has been held up as an argument for unlimited access to new reproductive technologies. Liberals see legal restrictions of the access to technology as paternalism. It should be up to the women themselves to choose whether they will use these technologies or not.

In this chapter I will attempt to give content to considerations such as continuity and interconnectedness in order to discuss these in the light of new reproductive technologies and reproductive freedom.

Continuity and Internal Reproduction

In her exposition of the political philosophy of birth, Mary O'Brien has brought out the existential values of maternity as continuous experience (O'Brien 1981). She has revealed the existential security and anchorage which the uninterrupted and continuous process of fertilization and pregnancy gives the woman compared with the man, whose reproductive experiences are seen as discontinuous and fragmented. In the process experienced by women, an integration of woman/nature and woman/child takes place. Also an integration in time takes place between generations which women experience themselves to be a physical and mental part of. The certainty that the child is her own links her directly to the offspring and to human continuity in the form of history.

Legally, the continuity consideration is rooted in family law, adoption law, inheritance law and in the institution of allodial rights. In most western countries the child's continuity in the sense of knowing his or her genetic origin is deeply rooted in the legal system. The Norwegian Adoption Act s.12(2) gives an adopted child at the age of 18 the right to know who his or her biological parents are. According to the Norwegian Children Act s.10(1), when a child is born out of marriage the District Governor has a duty to refer the case to court in order to establish paternity if the alleged father does not admit paternity.

For men, these laws have served as a means of creating a link to the mother and child and a link with the next generation. The "pater est" rule, the rule that the woman's husband is *prima facie* assumed to be the father of her child may be seen as an expression of men's need for existential continuity.

As regards maternity, the situation has been different. Maternity has, unlike paternity, been a reality, not a legal fiction. There has in Norwegian law not been any express statutory regulation of maternity. Norwegian law is considered to be based on a biological principle: the legal mother is the woman who bears the child (Backer 1982: 27, Stabel 1988). Woman's continuity is, as described by Mary O'Brien, closely linked to the reproductive process and directly experienced. We may here talk about the internal mode of reproduction as one where there is no gap between basis and superstructure.

External Fertilization, Continuity and Reproductive Freedom

External fertilization made possible by *in vitro* fertilization, egg donation and embryo donation disrupts the physical continuity of maternity:

- *In vitro* fertilization (IVF) refers to a noncoital way of conception which takes place outside the woman's body. A ripe human egg is extracted from the ovary, shortly before it would have been released naturally. Next the egg is mixed with the semen of the woman's partner, so that fertilization can occur. The fertilized egg is then transferred back to the woman's uterus.
- Egg donation is a procedure which may be used when the woman herself cannot produce eggs or is a bearer of hereditary diseases. An egg from a fertile woman is fertilized by semen from the infertile woman's partner *in vitro* and is transferred to the uterus of the infertile woman.
- Embryo donation involves the donation of both egg and semen. This is a possible solution when both the man and the woman are bearers of hereditary diseases or are infertile. The donated eggs are fertilized *in vitro* by donated semen and transferred to the uterus of the infertile woman.

Physically and conceptually motherhood has become a discontinuous process. A dividing line has been drawn between the egg and the womb. Eggs can be removed from the woman's ovaries to be fertilized, used as donation or frozen and stored for later use. The process of reproduction can be divided into component processes where elements can be removed, combined and replaced by medical experts. A distinction is now drawn between three types of maternity:

- the genetic mother: the woman who supplies the egg
- the biological mother: the woman who goes through the pregnancy and bears the child
- the social mother: the woman who takes care of the child.

Legally, the physical discontinuity has created doubt regarding motherhood. Who is the child's mother – the woman who donated the egg or the woman who bears the child? Technically, the problems created by this new situation may be solved by legislation. In England the Report of the Committee of Inquiry into Human Fertilisation and Embryology (Warnock 1985) in its list of recommendations suggests:

> 54. Legislation should provide that when a child is born to a woman following donation of another's egg the woman giving birth should, for all purposes, be regarded in law as the mother of that child, and that the egg donor should have no rights and obligations in respect of the child.

The physical discontinuity of maternity created by new reproductive technologies is, however, not only a technical problem, but also a moral and ethical one. Seen as a moral problem, one question is which values the legal regulation of *in vitro* fertilization, egg donation and embryo donation should be based on.

As mentioned, the approach of feminist philosophical, ethical and political trends which have an entire outlook on conception, pregnancy and birth and which are concerned with maternity as a basis for central human and social values has developed an understanding that will lead to decisive emphasis being placed on continuity factors in the context of legislative policy; from the present and the future – in the form of knowledge of her genetic offspring and as a responsibility for the life she has physically contributed to bringing into the world. The continuity principle entails regarding the human being as a responsible individual with roots in the present, the past and the future. The regard for continuity also embraces the interconnection in the environment where nature, the body, experiences and cultural values constitute an integrated whole.

At the Women's Emergency Conference on the New Reproductive Technologies in Vällinge, Sweden 1985, it was stated by the participants in the resolution passed:

> We want to maintain the integrity and embodiment of women's procreativity. Externalization of conception and gestation facilitates manipulation and genetic control. The division, fragmentation and separation of the female body into distinct parts for its scientific recombination disrupts historical continuity and identity. The individual becomes the dividual, the divided one.

In the discussion of moral values and legislative policy in this area, the community values of maternity and continuity should be evaluated in the light of the experiences and values of individual involuntarily childless women. One focal value which has been asserted is regard for reproductive freedom, including self-realization and self-determination of individual involuntarily childless women.

The legal scientist John A. Robertson represents a classical liberal approach towards infertility, reproductive technology and reproductive freedom. In his article (Robertson 1983) he gives the following definition of reproductive freedom: "Full reproductive freedom would include both freedom not to reproduce and to reproduce, when, with whom, and by what means one chooses."

In Robertson's opinion:

> Claims of protective freedom are logically extended to every aspect of reproduction: Conception, gestation, and childbearing. Although these components combine to create a powerful experience, each of them has a personal meaning independent of the others. For example it is meaningful to say that one has reproduced when one has merely passed on genes and neither gestated nor reared the resulting child. A gene contributor may find genetic transfer a vital source of feelings connecting him or her with nature and future generations.

Robertson further asserts: "Each aspect of reproduction can thus be a separate source of fulfilment and significance. Procreative freedom includes the right to separate genetic, gestational, or social components and to recombine them in collaboration with others."

One objection to this method of consideration is that it does not embrace the existential and emotional aspects of human reproduction. It rests on a mechanical and reductionist view of humanity. The view of egg donation as merely the donation of "genetic material" implies an application of the logic of the machine on human relations. By regarding egg donation merely as a donation of genetic material, human reproduction is considered as an act without direct moral responsibility for the child which will eventually come into the world. The responsibility is left with the receiver of the egg. It conflicts with both the principle of continuity and human dignity that the freedom to conceive and responsibility for conceiving should be divided.

As mechanical, abstract and alienated, the liberal concept of reproductive freedom may also be understood as a male-biased concept originating from men's discontinuous and fragmented reproductive experiences. For a man, it is physically and legally possible to evade parenthood. Women have had no such choice. Fatherhood also represents, unlike motherhood, a positive choice. Unlike motherhood, it is legally linked to social factors. A man may become a father by being married to the mother or by declaring he is the father of the child. In law motherhood has, as mentioned earlier, been based on a biological principle. For women, giving life and taking responsibility for life has been closely linked in body, life and law.

There are many examples of official legal policy based on liberty or equality considerations taking male biology as a point of departure. In the considerations of the Report of the Committee of Inquiry into Human Fertilisation and Embryology (Warnock 1985), the main reason given for the ethical and moral recognition of egg donation is equality considerations taking artificial insemination by donor as the point of departure.

> In weighing up the arguments for and against egg donation we have concluded that since we have accepted AID and IVF it would be illogical not to accept egg donation, notwithstanding the relatively minor surgical risks to the donor, inherent in egg recovery. We consider that egg donation is ethically acceptable where the donor has been properly counselled and is fully aware of the risks. It is both logical and consistent that the law should treat egg donation in the same way as AID and that the same principles of practice described in Chapter Four should apply to both.

In Denmark, the government committee which has reported on the need for regulation within the fields of gene splicing, test-tube fertilization, insemination, and foetus examinations, "Fremskridtets Pris", concludes that it sees no difference between insemination by donor (AID) and egg donation and therefore sees no objection against egg donation.

In my opinion, legal regulation should not take equality considerations based on male biology and values as a point of departure. It is not desirable that motherhood becomes more like fatherhood, external, discontinuous and fragmented. It will conflict with the child's as well as women's continuity and human dignity to consider them as suppliers of genetic material, cut off from both knowledge of and responsibility for the life they have chosen to be the origin of. In order to preserve the identity and dignity of human life, it is my view that legislation should link together giving of life and the taking of responsibility for life. Legislation should attach decisive importance to the regard for the continuity of childhood, maternity and paternity when striking a balance in terms of how the individual freedom should be defined in this field.

One example of official legal policy emphasizing continuity

considerations is the Norwegian Act relating to Artificial Procreation. The Act has a prohibition against egg donation, based on the biological and existential differences between maternity and paternity (s.12). Moreover, Norwegian legislation attaches decisive importance to regard for the child's continuity. The prohibition of egg donation is primarily justified by due consideration of the child, which is otherwise assumed to lose the most fundamental identity link it has through knowing for certain who the mother is.

Interconnectedness and Internal Reproduction

When it comes to the management of pregnancy, the maternal/foetal relation has basically been seen as interconnected in feminist theory, politics and law.

In 1915, the Norwegian author and politician, Katti Anker Möller, wrote *The Liberation of Motherhood* (Möller 1974) in which she gave the following description of the maternal/foetal relation:

> In the reproductive process – we are the whole and all the work – we nourish the foetus with our blood, we give it our strength – if we die, the foetus is going to die. No relation is more intimate – no possession more moral. We risk our life for its existence. But our existence is basic. The foetus cannot exist without us. Our power and our responsibility is given by nature.

In Norwegian as in most western legal systems, the foetus and the pregnant woman are basically treated as a legal unit. The Norwegian Abortion Act recognizes the interconnectedness between the foetus and the mother in laying down the principle that an abortion can be decided by the mother and only by her.

This principle is also integrated in the Working Environment Act, which aims at protecting the foetus by protecting the pregnant mother from various kinds of working conditions which may affect the health of the foetus.

Also health services and health law aim at securing healthy pregnancies and healthy babies. In this respect it is recognized that the final moral and legal responsibility for the child's health rests with the mother. In Norwegian law, prenatal diagnosis or medical intervention in the form of surgery on the foetus requires the consent of the mother.

The view of the maternal/foetal relation as closely interconnected is also in line with women's experiences as childbearers.

External Management of Pregnancy, Interconnectedness and Reproductive Freedom

External management and control of pregnancy is made possible by various forms of prenatal diagnosis and foetal medicine has made the foetus an object of medical observation, treatment and research through intervention in the body of the woman:

- Prenatal diagnosis refers to a variety of prenatal screening tests which can provide information about the likelihood of conceiving a child with a genetic defect. Prenatal tests can provide certain information about the health of the foetus. They range from non-intrusive techniques such as the visualizing of the foetus by sonography, to direct intrusions such as the sampling of the mother's amniotic fluid, drawing samples of foetal blood through a needle inserted in the uterus. These tests will also provide information about the child's sex.
- Foetal medicine is a new medical discipline focusing on the foetus as a patient. Until recently prenatal diagnosis offered only the option of abortion to women whose foetuses were discovered to have severe defects. Now some conditions can be treated *in utero* by administering drugs to the mother and by intervening surgically through foetoscopy.

In medical theory, separateness rather than interconnectedness is emphasized in the description of the maternal foetal relation. At the Second International Symposium on the Foetus as a Patient – Diagnosis and Treatment in Jerusalem in 1985, the moderator of the round-table discussion on the ethical, legal and religious aspects of the modern diagnostic and therapeutic approach to the foetus defined the problem as follows:

> Now that the foetus is a visible, vivid object of diagnosis and therapy, it is evident that the mother and foetus are not a single biological entity, but two distinct patients. If the foetus is a distinct human, does it not thereby deserve the right to be treated? Does the foetus have a new moral status by virtue of the new therapeutic option available to it? Does the right of the foetus to be treated override the right of the mother who rejects the new modalities of foetal therapy? (Schenker & Weinstein 1986).

It is argued that the physical separation of the mother and the foetus for the first time in history gives women a positive reproductive choice. The choice she has had so far, provided by contraception and abortion, has been negative. By providing information on the health of the foetus and improving the possibilities of medical management and control, pregnancy is no longer doomed to biological destiny. Modern medicine has provided alternatives.

Whether women's reproductive freedom will be strengthened or promoted by the modernization of pregnancy by externalization, separation and medicalization is in my view a complex question which depends on factors such as the legal, political, religious, social economic and cultural context.

Legal Principles and Values as Context

The legal context of these new reproductive technologies is an important factor providing the formal conditions of reproductive freedom.

The principle of women's reproductive freedom is to a varying degree rooted in the legal systems of the western world. The principle of reproductive freedom embraces the bodily, personal and reproductive integrity:

- The principle of bodily integrity means that physical intervention in the woman's body cannot take place without her consent.
- The principle of personal integrity means that information about the woman should not be gathered or given without her consent.
- The principle of reproductive integrity recognizes that the relationship with the foetus is mediated by the mother. Legally the ethical and moral responsibility rests with the mother. An example is abortion laws leaving the decision whether an abortion should take place or not to the mother.

These principles are, as earlier illustrated, closely connected with an outlook on the maternal/foetal relation as closely interconnected, and on maternity as charged with moral and ethical responsibility.

The minimum requirement of women's reproductive freedom is that these formal principles are maintained and developed in the legal regulation of new reproductive technologies.

Legal Principles and Values in Context

The legal system with its principles and values is not static. Law is an open system which is subject to a continuous process of change. The process of law may be seen as interplay between law, medicine, politics, culture, social organization and economy.

In the reproductive sphere, the interplay between the legal principles of bodily, personal and reproductive integrity, medical technologies, practices and definitions, politics, culture and social organizations ought to be studied in order to evaluate whether women's reproductive freedom is promoted or undermined by new reproductive technologies. There are likely to be great variations in terms of cultural, legal, political and social differences in different countries.

Using randomly chosen examples from the United States and India, I will briefly illustrate how externalization of management and control of pregnancy may affect some of the principles.

A: The principle of bodily integrity may be undermined by medical theory and practice if supported by political factors.

In the United States, changes in legal practice influenced by changes in medical theory and practice have been observed. Court-ordered obstetrical procedures are growing in number. A national survey investigating the scope and circumstances of court-ordered obstetrical procedures in cases where women had refused therapy deemed necessary for the foetus by the doctor shows that court orders have been obtained for caesarian section in eleven states, hospital detention in two states, and intra-uterine transfer in one state. The investigation showed it was a widely held view among heads of fellowship programmes in maternal/foetal medicine that women who refused medical advice and thereby endangered the life of the foetus should be detained (Kolder et al. 1987).

The right to bodily integrity grounded in common-law principles explicitly articulated in the doctrine of consent is frequently debated in American legal theory. The medical definition of the foetus as a person and of the maternal/foetal relation as one of two separate persons with conflicting interests has influenced many leading legal scholars. One example is the viewpoint of John A. Robertson (1983):

> The more difficult question would be whether the therapy could be directly imposed on her against her will. Would her interest in bodily integrity override the unborn child's interest in life and health? Bodily intrusions for the sake of another are highly disfavoured, but are not unknown to the law. If the risk to the mother is slight and the benefit to the child is great, there are precedents that will authorize a court to order treatment against

> the mother's will. In Raleigh Fitkin – Paul Morgan Memorial Hospital versus Andersom, the New Jersey Supreme Court ordered blood transfusions against the wishes of a Jehovah's witness whose severe hemorrhaging threatened her life and that of her eight month old fetus. More recently, the Georgia Supreme Court ordered that a cesarean section be performed on a full-term woman who refused it on religious grounds and who had complete placenta previa, a condition almost certain to cause her death and the death of the fetus.
>
> These cases allow direct bodily intrusions to benefit a viable, full-term fetus when the risks that the intervention poses for the mother are reasonable. Although these cases involved saving both the fetus and the mother's life, they lay the foundation for requiring a pregnant woman to permit in utero foetal therapy essential to the health or survival of a viable fetus, so long as the therapy does not pose substantial threats to her life or health.

Robertson also discusses the possibilities of making prenatal tests mandatory:

> Prenatal diagnosis could be mandated indirectly by imposing tort liability on women whose failure to use it results in harm to their children. In Grodin versus Grodin the court recognized a child's right to sue its mother for failure to obtain a pregnancy test. The rationale of this decision suggests that a child may also sue his mother for failing to monitor her pregnancy in order to discover and correct threats to the fetus's health.
>
> Prenatal screening could also be directly mandated by statute, with criminal penalties for the woman who fails to obtain it. State authorities could justify such a statute on public health grounds as being necessary to inform women of their fetus's health.

As illustrated, there is a trend in medical theory and practice supported in legal practice and theory of giving the foetus status as a separate patient whose interests should under certain circumstances be given greater priority than the mother's interest of bodily integrity. These viewpoints are, however, very controversial both legally and morally.

In their extreme, such opinions represent a view of women as vessels and "means to an end" denied the responsibility and bodily integrity which is specific to human dignity in western democratic societies. The tendency of regarding women as bearers of healthy babies for the community denied individual bodily integrity bears a resemblance to Nazi birth law. In Nazi birth law, the communal interest in genetically, socially and racially healthy babies was given greater priority than the personal, bodily and reproductive integrity of the individual women. To promote these goals, forced sterilization and forced abortion was mandated by law.

B: The principles of integrity may also be undermined by the interplay between reproductive technology, cultural, social and economic factors.

An Indian woman who was married to a business man had an abortion when she heard the result of a prenatal test showing the sex of the foetus. The pressure on her by her husband and his family to have a sex determination test was great.

> You just do not know what I have been going through in the last seven years because all I gave birth to were girls! Again and again it is a girl, I carry her for nine months. The family prays to God, the priest pays a visit, the family undertakes puja (a religious ceremony). Then the day arrives, the labour starts. Then finally the birth. And again nothing. After my second and third delivery all they did was to send my little brother-in-law to see me at the hospital. It would be so much easier for me with a son. My husband and my family would respect me so much more (Roggenkamp 1984).

In this case, the interplay between technology and patriarchal cultural and social forces can be seen as undermining the principles of reproductive integrity and self-determination. The preference for sons in middle and upper casts in northern and western India has been explained by factors such as patriarchal ownership of land and property, the patriarchal family structure and the dowry which has to be paid by the bride's family (Kishwar 1985). Widowhood, separation and divorce – all of which exclude women from sources of income – have also been pointed to as an explanation of women's son preference. Sons are seen as an important source of insurance against the risk of losing the economic support of a husband (Cain 1984).

Conclusion

The values of continuity and interconnectedness may, as illustrated in this chapter, conflict with the consideration of reproductive freedom in the sense of positive reproductive choice in the form of unlimited access to new reproductive technologies such as *in vitro* fertilization, prenatal tests and perinatal medicine. As illustrated, new reproductive technologies may also under certain social, political and cultural conditions undermine the principles of personal, bodily and reproductive integrity and basic legal conditions for reproductive freedom.

Emphasizing continuity and interconnectedness between nature, body and mind in the evaluation of external reproduction by means of complicated technology and professional assistance is on the other hand in line with the "organic" concept of freedom on which Ivan Illich builds his model for a community based on a proper balance between nature and technology (Illich 1977). He stresses the need for a process and methodology as a step towards identifying the fundamental values that lead to freedom, self-determination and self-realization and those which on the other hand lead to the furtherance of technological obsession in the form of relations of dominance and subordination. Ivan Illich emphasizes the independent and creative intercourse between human beings, free individual development, and a balance between humanity and development. In this connection he distinguishes between tools made to suit human bodily power and rhythm and advanced technological tools that dictate the rhythm and the pattern of human relations.

Note

* This article was first published under the title "Law and Modern Technology" in *High-Technology and Law: A Critical Approach* A. Sajo (ed.). Institute of Political and Legal Sciences, Budapest 1989.

7

New Reproductive Technology in an Ecological Perspective*

ANNE HELLUM

Reproductive Technology and Utopias

Technology that can direct natural processes such as fertilization, pregnancy and birth is a recurring theme in the fancies of modern authors, scientists and politicians about the ideal society of the future. The wish to be able to decide everything, from how many children, to what kind of children, and how they are to be conceived and born, is part of the vision of the future depicted by radical feminists, socialists and nazis alike. Technology that can control unrestrained and uncontrollable natural fertility is described both in optimistic sketches of a liberated society and in pessimistic, nightmarish descriptions of regimes with absolute and total control.

The Dream of a Genderless Society

To the radical feminist Shulamit Firestone, a prerequisite for liberation and equality between the sexes is the separation of fertility from gender and body (Firestone 1970). In her book *The Dialectic of Sex* she paints a picture of a society where gender is of no importance. Modern reproductive technology in the form of *in vitro* fertilization and an artificial womb have liberated women from biological motherhood. Fertilization, pregnancy and birth are not regarded as an enriching experience but as the root of suffering, misery and suppression. Only when liberated from the burden of motherhood can women develop their abilities in the fields of science, art and politics, as men have always done.

In Aldous Huxley's nightmarish society *Brave New World*, both biological reproduction and social reproduction are the responsibility of the State (Huxley 1985). Children are produced artificially and are cared for in public institutions. The adults live alone, without caring for each other and with no responsibility for each other. Family, sexuality and love are forbidden. People are not allowed to develop personal relationships, they must relate only to Big Brother, the authoritarian state.

The Genetically Ideal Society

The growth of eugenics as a new scientific discipline in the United States and Europe in the 1920s gave rise to dreams of the elimination of poverty and suffering by improving the genetic material of the human race. The eugenicist Julian Huxley, brother of Aldous Huxley, envisaged a eugenically ideal society. He saw eugenics as a tool which human beings and science could use to shape a radiant genetic future. In an article in *Harper's Magazine* in 1931 he summed up his visions as follows:

> We cannot yet see what those discoveries will be, or envisage the future of the eugenic society. But knowledge will slowly grow, ways and means can surely be found. And so man may take up his birthright, which is to become the first organism exercising conscious control over its own evolutionary destiny (Huxley 1931).

In the birth policy of the nazis, the utopia of the eugenic society was implemented in practical politics. Control of the quality and quantity of the population occurred through the controlling of women. The legislation contained both direct and indirect coercion (Brase 1981, Aasen 1989). One instrument of family policy was a loan upon marriage. Such a loan was granted on the basis of a genetic, social and racial assessment of the couple. The genetic material of the population was charted. Legislation on abortion and sterilization provided the authority to intervene by force in the lives of mentally deranged, anti-social, idle or handicapped persons. In Germany, this authority to use coercion was actually applied and a number of women died after forced abortions and sterilization under unsanitary conditions. In nazi ideology and juridical thinking it was society that counted and not the individual. As far as the birth policy was concerned, this meant that principles of justice such as self-determination and autonomy had to give way to the public interest in achieving a racially pure society.

Reproductive Technology and Ecology

Today's technological developments have to a large extent passed the bounds of utopia. In the field of medical research, developments have been explosive. Natural processes are no longer inextricably linked to the female body, but have become severed from it both in time and space.

Today, in the case of fertilization, pregnancy and birth, a woman is offered a wide range of medical/technological services comprising everything from artificial fertilization in the form of insemination by donor (AID) to *in vitro* fertilization (IVF). Fertilization is possible using donated semen, eggs or embryo. Eggs, semen and embryo can be frozen and stored. Ultrasound, amniocentesis and tests on the placenta are new techniques that have been developed with a view to discovering birth defects at an early stage of pregnancy. Prenatal medicine is a new branch of medicine with the objective of discovering and treating disorders of the embryo within the womb. Genetic engineering makes it possible to influence a person's genes by manipulating somatic cells and germ cells.

Parallel with these rapid developments in medical science is the ever-approaching threat of the destruction of nature and the world itself through the disturbance of the environment. Pollution of the natural environment causes not only damage to forests, and mutations and reduced fertility in certain animal species. It also affects human fertility and genetic material. Today, scientists and environmental activists are devoting increasing attention to the connection between environmental pollution and birth defects, spontaneous abortion and infertility.

About thirty–forty children are born in Norway each year with birth defects caused by chemical substances and products. The extent of other damage, such as damage to the genetic material, after exposure to chemicals is not known.

A number of studies indicate that men's fertility has decreased during the last twenty years (Osser et al. 1984; Busund & Bendvold 1988). This is due to a reduction in the quality of their semen. For example, many studies show that the semen contains fewer "swimmers", thus reducing fertility levels. Scientists are asking whether this situation could be caused by pollution and industrialization. One Swedish study shows greater changes in urban areas than in the country (Osser et al. 1984).

In Poland's largest industrial area, Katowices (also called "The Triangle of Death"), the situation is dramatic. Every second child in the area is born with defects caused by pollution. Doctors advise young people in the area not to marry another person from the same district because of the very high risk of giving birth to children with defects. In an interview printed in the Danish newspaper *Information* on 23 January 1990, a Polish professor of medicine, who is also a member of Poland's ecological society, said: "When one is faced with two pregnant women in a doctor's consulting rooms it is beyond bearing to think that one of them will give birth to a handicapped child."

The department for premature babies in Zabrze has stated that thirty per cent of all pregnancies in the area end in abortion before the 28th week, ten per cent of the babies are born before the 27th week, ten per cent are born underweight with a handicap, and only fifty per cent are born with no problems at all.

The accident in Chernobyl has prompted studies into the connection between birth defects and the environment in a number of European countries (Ulstein et al. 1990). In Norway, the number of spontaneous abortions increased after the accident, but not the number of legal abortions. There was an increase in the number of legal abortions in Denmark and Greece after the accident, most likely due to fear of birth defects. The radiation following a nuclear accident is usually divided into two components, external radiation which strikes the body from outside and internal radiation which is absorbed through food etc. It is assumed that internal radiation is the most important component that affects biological reproduction.

In her book *No Immediate Danger*, Rosalie Bertell has charted the relationship between radiation from nuclear power plants and nuclear explosions in Europe, the United States and Asia and the effects it has on fertility and inheritable material (Bertell 1985). She is not only concerned with the consequences of the dramatic accidents. Bertell shows that it may well be the "mild mutations", the small genetic changes that are neither measured nor discussed, that represent the greatest threat to the future of mankind. According to Bertell, changes in the genetic material take place within the framework of the permitted level of radiation. Over a number of generations the genetic material will be affected, and people will become less immune.

Choice of Values

In a global and long-term perspective, man's ability to reproduce new generations is becoming increasingly threatened. There is a need for action.

One alternative is to try to repair the damage that has been caused by technological intervention in natural processes and fertility over many years. Egg banks and semen banks make it possible to preserve good genetic material. This can be distributed through the public health services or by buying and selling. Artificial insemination with donated eggs and semen can be offered to persons living in areas where they are exposed to pollution and radiation. Egg banks, semen banks and artificial insemination can also be coupled to genetic guidance, and in the future may become a positive alternative to prenatal diagnostics and selective abortion.

A second alternative is the ecological approach. This is associated with a different medical tradition than the technologically innovative approach, namely with preventive or environmental medicine (Grandjean 1988). Within this tradition, doctors have begun to accept their role in the fight against environmental degradation. The focus is on preventing infertility and birth defects through primary health services in the working environment and the natural environment.

In the short term, repairing damage by means of advanced medical technology gives quicker and greater benefit than prevention of the damage through measures in the field of environmental health. Technology can be used to solve the problems of individual women. Prenatal diagnostics can show that a foetus is malformed, and the woman has an opportunity to choose abortion. *In vitro* fertilization gives childless women new hope. Ten–fifteen per cent of childless women who are treated with IVF become pregnant. Eliminating nuclear power plants and nuclear explosions, or reducing emissions of toxic gases takes more time and may seem an endless task. On the other hand, in contrast to technological solutions, which focus on symptoms rather than causes, prevention of infertility and birth defects through environmental health measures strike at the root of the problem.

The choice between technology and ecology is not only a matter of finding effective and practical solutions. It concerns a choice of values and one's view of mankind. The terms *rationality of responsibility* and *limited technical rationality* may help to clarify the different choices of values and ideologies that are implicit in the two approaches: the technological and the ecological perspectives (Ve 1990).

Technology and Control

Limited technical rationality originates from capitalistic production and is characterized by regarding human beings not as a goal in themselves but as a means of achieving the goals for production. In the context of human fertilization this implies that the natural processes, fertilization, pregnancy and birth, are not regarded as a goal in themselves but as means to something else, e.g. career, scientific insight or economic profit. The body and the natural processes are perceived as a means of production, a kind of machine that can be controlled.

All the imagined utopias – from that of the extreme feminist Shulamit Firestone to that of Julian Huxley – are based on the ideals of self-realization and freedom that originated in the Age of Enlightenment. The ideal of man's realization of self is applied in relation to the body, biology and the liberation of fertility from nature and fate. Both Shulamit Firestone and Simone de Beauvoir saw wild and uncontrollable fertility as the cause of women's lack of success in the fields of science, philosophy and art. In their view, the way to the higher intellectual spheres, to a large extent dominated by men, is closely connected to control of the body. Technology is necessary in order to transport women from the natural, primitive level where consciousness is controlled by bodily forces to a higher cultural level controlled by thoughts and intellect. Firestone's dream that an artificial womb would liberate women from physical work and thus allow intellectual work is an extreme expression of limited technical rationality.

Limited technical rationality is what characterizes to an extreme degree the social, economic and legal principles governing the new reproductive technology in the United States. Fertilization, pregnancy and birth have become a means of profit. The principle of freedom of contract also applies almost without limitations to fertility. Eggs, semen and embryos can be bought and sold. The private health services earn millions of dollars from fertilizing childless women. An increasing number of working-class women make a living by hiring out their wombs to rich childless couples. In such cases the wife is often either unable to have a child or does not wish to complete a pregnancy for career reasons.

Technical rationality is not as prominent in Norway where, for example, the Act relating to Artificial Procreation limits the extent to which the process of fertilization can be exploited for reasons of profit or for the purposes of research (s.3). By forbidding the purchasing and selling of eggs and semen, donation of eggs and embryos, and contracts with surrogate mothers, Norwegian legislation attempts to protect the natural processes from commercialization. By prohibiting research on fertilized eggs, the Act further protects against experiments on life and manipulation of life (s.3(3)). Life is protected from being used as a way to obtain more knowledge. Nor does the Act make artificial procreation a right for the individual, as many childless couples or women maintain. Juridically speaking, artificial procreation is a public health service that is limited to childless married couples (ss.4 and 5).

Many women think that the new reproductive technology is a positive development, and that women should have a greater right to fertilization. In Norway, the Association of Childless Persons has demanded that childlessness should be given legal status as a disease. A demand has been put forward for fair and non-discriminating distribution of artificial procreation as a public health service. The extreme is expressed in the following slogan from 8 March: "Single women and lesbian women demand the right to artificial insemination."

Many women politicians and scholars engaged in women's studies dissociate themselves entirely from the rights-oriented, optimistic view of technology. One woman who rejects this optimism is the author Gena Corea. In her book *The Mother Machine* she rejects every form of modern reproductive technology because it regards the female body and the fertility process as parts of a machine that can be replaced and manipulated (Corea 1985). The female body and the natural process of fertility become an object for capitalistic expansion through the transition from mechanical to organic production. According to Maria Mies, the female body is "the last colony" (Mies 1986).

"We are our bodies, we are our eggs" was the slogan of opponents of the new genetic and reproductive technology when they assembled at the First European Feminist Conference Against Genetic and Reproductive Technology in Majorca in 1987. The conference was arranged by FINRAGE (Feminist International Network Against Reproductive and Genetic Engineering). With this slogan they denied the dichotomy between body and soul, and between fertility and the body. The conference resulted in a demand for a considerate and caring medical approach to infertility and birth defects, based on the unity of body and soul, and of man and nature.

Ecology and Caring

The rationality of responsibility or the rationality of caring perceives human life as a goal in itself. A fundamental value is to take care of all life. The philosopher Nell Noddings has developed an ethics of caring that is based on everyday relationships between people, between people and animals and between people and plants (Noddings 1984).[1]

Ivan Illich's ecologically-oriented concept of freedom is closely linked to the ethics of caring in its broadest sense, and represents the opposite to Shulamit Firestone's ideal of freedom through technology. In his book *Tools for Conviviality* he makes a distinction between technology which leads to self-realization and liberation, and technology which leads to exclusion, subordination and dependence. He deliberates on the difference between tools and instruments which work in accord with the rhythm of the body and the biological urges, and those which work against and dominate both these and interpersonal relationships (Illich 1977).

Environmental medicine is a product of an ethics which reflects care for all life, whether it be animal life, human life or plant life. Human fertility and new life is regarded as threatened, along with the rest of nature. Man is perceived as part of nature. Protection of human fertility and life go hand in hand with protection of nature.

The concept of man as part of nature is also expressed in women's studies based on eastern philosophy. In her book *Staying Alive*, the Indian philosopher and physicist Vandana Shiva points to the separation of man and nature as a characteristic of the western scientific tradition which started with Francis Bacon (Shiva 1988). She considers the global environmental crisis in relation to this scientific standpoint, which conceives nature as "environment" or "a resource". According to Shiva, when the environment is regarded as separate from man, as the surroundings of man and not his substance, then man has allowed himself to subjugate nature. This assumption has given food to a world view where nature is inert and passive, uniform and mechanistic, separable and fragmented within itself, separate and inferior, something to be dominated and exploited by man. Shiva compares this world view with the opposing idea of the cosmos. This regards man and nature, male and female, as two sides of a dialectical harmony. All existence originates from a dialectic interplay between creation and dissolution, interrelationship and dissolution. Out of the tension that is created by this process comes Prakriti, conceived as developing and expanding nature. The diversity which Prakriti produces is expressed in the common, and yet multiple, life of the mountains, trees, rivers and animals. The creative force and the created world are not separate and distinct, but dynamic and interrelated. According to Vandana Shiva, Prakriti is an everyday concept which people use to organize their daily life. It provides a basis for ecological thinking and action.

One of the most fundamental works within the western scientific tradition, Darwin's *On the Origin of Species by Means of Natural Selection; or the Preservation of Favoured Races in the Struggle for Life*, is interpreted by modern researchers in literature and the social sciences as a work which emphasizes human beings as being part of nature, not superior and dominating as indicated by Bacon (Ryall 1990). The *Origin* is read as a substitute to the biblical view of the world, with its potentially equally all-embracing system. In contrast to the *Bible*, the *Origin* is conceived as an open system, without any Divine control or initiation. Instead, it describes nature as a creative force. Change and development are a result of "natural selection", that is to say non-human and unintentional priority selection of specific properties over thousands of generations. Man is therefore dethroned, and becomes a small part of the large and complex whole. The world view depicted in the *Origin* does not place man at the top of a hierarchy, nor does it separate man from nature.

Environmental law as a juridical discipline is based on a distinction between man and nature. Man is conceived as a user of nature, not as a direct part of nature in the same way as animals and plants. The concept of nature in environmental law, as defined by Inge Lorange Backer in his thesis *Nature Conservation and Intervention in Nature*, raises in the first place legal questions referring to the so-called classical concept of nature conservation, implying conservation of specific areas including plants, animals and landscapes, and protection of specific species (Backer 1986). Secondly, it raises, with certain limitations, questions connected to the ecologically sound management of natural resources. The term environmental considerations includes taking into account resources, pollution, conservation of land, and the urban environment. The main actors in environmental law are the violators of the environment and the conservers of the environment. The violators are those who interfere in the environment and the conservers are those who agitate to conserve and maintain the environment. Man is not included in the enumeration of the forms of life and the species to which the concept of nature conservation refers. Nor is consideration for human health, including the ability to create new life through fertilization, included in the list of environmental considerations. Man is regarded as a user, either as a violator or a conserver, and as a threatening and not a threatened species.

A "neither/nor" approach to the relationship between man and nature might give more weight and greater reach to environmental considerations. Such an approach implies combining the two approaches discussed above and regarding man as both a user of nature and as a part of nature, in the same way as animals and plants. This implies directly including not only the intrinsic value of nature but also of man. This is practised in birth law, a juridical discipline that takes up the legal aspects of the birth process in the broadest sense: fertilization, pregnancy, birth and care (Fastvold 1990).

In this connection, respect for natural processes and caring for the individual and coming generations, are two fundamental values which emphasize the interplay between man and nature. Consideration for coming generations has been developed, for example, with a view to integrating consideration for children and caring in the planning legislation. This is illustrated by the following analogy between the child welfare service and nature conservation, obtained by "rewriting" the Nature Conservation Act:

> Children are a national asset which must be protected. Protection of children means the management of child resources based on an acknowledgement of the close inter-relationship between man and nature, and on the preservation of the quality of children for the future. All persons shall show due consideration and care in their contacts with children. Child planning should only be undertaken on the basis of long-term and comprehensive management of resources providing for the preservation of childhood and children in the future as a basis for human activity, health and well-being (Fastvold 1990).

Consideration for the protection of human health as part of nature has gradually gained some footing in Norwegian legislation. The Working Environment Act, the Municipal Health Services Act, the Pollution Control Act, the Nuclear Energy Act and the Nature Conservation Act all contain rules which emphasize the relationship between human health and the social and natural environment. The Municipal Health Services Act defines environmental health measures as measures that refer to factors in the environment which may at any time directly or indirectly affect health. Such factors include biological, chemical, physical and social environmental factors.

In a global and long-term perspective, the ability of human beings to produce new generations is becoming increasingly threatened.

St. meld. no. 46 (1988–89) on Environment and Development, which describes the measures to be introduced in Norway to follow up the Report of the World Commission on Environment and Development, shows that the Government has started to take this dismal development seriously. It states that Norway will become the host country for a permanent international centre for information on the connection between environmental damage and birth defects. One purpose of the centre is to provide more knowledge about the effect of environmental problems on, *inter alia*, genetic material and development of the foetus, in order to prevent malformations. The basis for this centre will be laid in a three–four year pilot project which was started in 1989.

Sustainable Development

My reason for including the consideration for protection of fertility and life through environmentally-oriented health services into the discussion on the new reproductive technologies is a wish to emphasize the need for a holistic perspective, with the focus on caring for future generations. In other words, an ecological perspective, including charting the extent to which women's and men's fertility and the life of the embryo in the mother's body is, or should be, protected against external environmental impacts in actual fact and by law. In my opinion this should be an important subsidiary goal in relation to the primary objective of the Brundtland Commission: "sustainable development".

Notes

* This article was first published in Beatrice Halsaa and Else Viestad (eds.). *I pose og sekk. Framtidsbilder* (To Have it Both Ways. Visions for the Future). Oslo: Emilia Press, 1990.

1 Lis Frost has analyzed the new reproductive technologies in the light of an ethics of rights and an ethics of care (Frost 1989).

Bibliography

Agerup, Anita 1990. *Om Straffeutmåling i voldtektssaker med særlig vekt på psykiske skader for ofrene* (Sentencing in Rape Cases). Thesis in Law. Kvinnerettslige Arbeidsnotater nr. 47. Institute of Women's Law, University of Oslo.

Amundsen, Arne Bugge 1983. *Dåp og tradisjon* (Baptism and Tradition). Oslo.

Andenæs, Johs 1971. *Spesiell strafferett* (Criminal Law: Special Part). Oslo: Universitetsforlaget.

Arditti, Rita, Renate D. Klein & Shelley Minden (eds.) 1984. *Test-tube Women: What Future for Motherhood?* London: Pandora Press.

Arms, Suzanne 1975. *Immaculate Deception. A New Look at Women and Childbirth in America.* Boston: San Francisco Book Company/Houghton Mifflin.

Arnholm, Carl Jacob & Peter Lødrup 1976. *Familieretten* (Family Law). Oslo: Tanum.

Backer, Inge Lorange 1982. *Barneloven. Kommentarutgave* (Children Act. A Commentary). Oslo: Universitetsforlaget.

Backer, Inge Lorange 1986. *Naturvern og naturinngrep* (Nature Conservation and Intervention in Nature). Oslo: Universitetsforlaget.

Belenky, Mary F., Blyth M. Clichy, Nancy R. Goldberger & Jill M. Tatule 1986. *Women's Ways of Knowing: The Development of Self, Voice and Mind.* New York: Basic Books.

Berg, Ulla et al. 1978. "Information och stöd till föräldrar som förlorat sitt barn ved födselen" (Information and Support to Parents who Lose their Child at Birth). *Läkartidningen*, Vol. 75, pp. 128–32.

Bertell, Rosalie 1985. *No Immediate Danger.* New York: The Women's Press.

Bjøro, Kristian 1987. "Prenatal Diagnostikk: Indikasjoner og metoder" (Prenatal Diagnosis: Indications and Methods). *Tidskrift for Den norske Lægeforening* nr. 14.

Borchgrevink, Mette 1979. "Livmorens juss og politikk" (Law and Politics Relating to the Womb). *Kvinnerettslige studier*, nr. 8. Institute of Women's Law, University of Oslo.

Brase, Kay Herman 1981. "Nazismen og den tyske kvinde, 1933–1945" (Nazism and German Women, 1933–1945). Manuscript. Department of History, University of Århus.

Bratholm, Anders 1969. *Umyndige personer* (Minors). Oslo: Universitetsforlaget.

Bull, Kirsti Strøm 1979. "Avtaler mellom ugifte samboende" (Agreements Between Unmarried Cohabitees). *Tidsskrift for rettsvitenskap*, pp. 82 f.

Bull, Kirsti Strøm 1982. "Hjemmearbeidets erstatningsrettslige stilling" (The Status of Housework in Tort Law). *Tidsskrift for Rettsvitenskap*, pp. 903 f.

Bull, Kirsti Strøm 1983. "Ugift samliv – noen synspunkter på rettsutviklingen i Sverige og Norge" (Unmarried Cohabitation – Thoughts on Legal Development in Sweden and Norway). *Tidsskrift for rettsvitenskap*, pp. 590 f.

Bull, Kirsti Strøm 1985a. "Dødfødsel og rettsplikt overfor foreldre" (Stillbirth and Parent's Legal Rights). *In* Tove Stang Dahl (ed.), *Kvinnerett I.* Oslo: Universitetsforlaget.

Bull, Kirsti Strøm 1985b. "Husmorens erstatningsrettslige stilling" (The Housewife's Position in Tort Law). *In* Tove Stang Dahl (ed.), *Kvinnerett II.* Oslo: Universitetsforlaget.

Bull, Kirsti Strøm 1990. *Ugift Samliv* (Unmarried Cohabitation). Oslo: Tano forlag.

Busund, Bjørn & Erik Bendvold 1988. "Mulig reduksjon i sædkvalitet i løpet av en 20-årsperiode" (Possible Reduction in Sperm Quality over a Twenty Year Period). *Tidskrift for Den norske Lægeforening*, nr. 5, pp. 403–4.

Bø, Olav 1960. "Øskjer i kyrkjemuren" (Boxes in the Church Wall). *Norveg*, pp. 99 f.

Cain, M. 1984. "Women's Status and Fertility in Developing Countries: Son Preference and Economic Security", *World Bank Staff Working Papers*.

Cedercreutz, Camilla 1989. *Moderskapet som kroppslig erfarenhet och det specifika vätandet som däri ligger* (Motherhood as a Physical Experience). Helsingfors: Sosial och hälsovårdsministeriet, Jämställdhetspublikationer, Serie D. nr. 3.

Chodorow, Nancy 1978. *The Reproduction of Mothering: Psychoanalysis and the Sociology of Gender*. Berkeley: University of California Press.

Christie, Nils 1989. *Bortenfor anstalt og ensomhet: Om landsbyer for usedavalige mennesker* (Beyond Institutions and Loneliness: Communes for Extraordinary People who are Different). Oslo: Universitetsforlaget. *Also in* Nils Christie *Beyond Loneliness and Institutions. Communes for Extraordinary People*. Oslo: Norwegian University Press.

Christie, Nils et al. (eds.) 1990. *...den urett som ikke rammer deg selv: Festskrift til Anders Bratholm, 70 år* (The Injustice that Does Not Affect You: Festschrift to Anders Bratholm). Oslo: Universitetsforlaget.

Church Council Working Group 1989, I. *Kirkerådet arbeidsgruppe*: Mer enn gener. Utredning om bioteknologi og menneskeverd, 1989 (More than Genes: A Report on Biotechnology and Human Worth). Oslo.

Church Council Working Group 1989, II. *Kirkerådets arbeidsgruppe*: Svangerskap og rettsvern. En betenkning om abortlovgivningen, 1989 (Pregnancy and Legal Protection: A Report on Abortion Legislation). Oslo.

Clarke, Michael & Anthony J. Williams 1979. "Depression in Women after Perinatal Death", *The Lancet*, pp. 916–7.

Clayman, Ronald I. et al. 1980. "Issues Concerning Parents after the Death of their Newborn", *Critical Care Medicine*, Vol. 8, pp. 215–8.

Corea, Gena 1985. *The Mother Machine: Reproductive Technologies from Artificial Insemination to Artificial Wombs*. New York: Harper & Row.

Cullberg, Johan 1966. "Reaktioner inför perinatal barnedöd (I): Psykiska följder hos kvinnan" (Reactions to Perinatal Child Death: Mental Consequences for the Woman). *Läkartidningen*, Vol. 63, pp. 3980–6. "Reaktioner inför perinatal barnadød (II): Förhållandet patient-läkare" (Reactions to Perinatal Child Death: The Patient-Doctor Relationship). *Läkartidningen*, Vol. 63, pp. 4065–8.

Dahl, Tove Stang 1982. "Kvinners rett til penger" (Women's Right to Money). *In* Haukaa et al. (eds.), *Kvinneforskning: Bidrag til samfunnsteori*. Oslo: Universitetsforlaget. *Also in* Tove Stang Dahl 1987. *Women's Law: An Introduction to Feminist Jurisprudence*. Oslo: Norwegian University Press.

Dahl, Tove Stang 1985a. "Diskriminering mellom arbeidsløse" (Discrimination Between the Unemployed). *In* Tove Stang Dahl (ed.), *Kvinnerett II*. Oslo: Universitetsforlaget. *Also in* Tove Stang Dahl 1987. *Women's Law. An Introduction to Feminist Jurisprudence*. Oslo: Norwegian University Press.

Dahl, Tove Stang 1985b. "Fra husmorrettens spesielle del: Folketrygdens regel om forhøyet hjelpestønad til funksjonshemmede barn" (Towards a Housewives Law). *In* Tove Stang Dahl (ed.) *Kvinnerett II*. Oslo: Universitetsforlaget. *Also in* Tove Stang Dahl 1987. *Women's Law. An Introduction to Feminist Jurisprudence*. Oslo: Norwegian University Press.

Dahl, Tove Stang 1987. *Women's Law: An Introduction to Feminist Jurisprudence*. Oslo: Norwegian University Press.

Dahl, Tove Stang 1990a. "Pene piker haiker ikke. Om bil som tvang til voldtekt." (Nice Girls Don't Hitch-Hike: The Motorcar in Forcible Rape). *In* Nils Christie et al. (eds.) ...*den urett som ikke rammer deg selv: Festskrift til Anders Bratholm, 70 år*. Oslo: Universitetsforlaget.

Dahl, Tove Stang 1990b. "Bargaining for Welfare: Control, Class and Gender. Lecture at the International Symposium Commemorating Vilhelm Aubert. Oslo: Institutt for samfunnsforskning.

Davies, D. P. 1983. "Support after Perinatal Death: A Study of Support and Counselling after Perinatal Bereavement," *British Medical Journal*, Vol. 286, pp. 144–5.

Eckhoff, Torstein 1978. *Forvaltningsrett* (Administrative Law). Oslo: Tanum.

Ehrenreich 1973.

Elster, Jon 1990. "Høyre eller venstre" (Right or Left). *Nytt Norsk Tidsskrift*, nr. 2.

Ertesvåg, Vera 1975. "Makt og avmakt. Begynnende faglig organisering av kvinnene" (Power and Powerlessness: Initial Trade Organization of Women). *Kjerringråd*, nr. 1.

Ethical Considerations of the New Reproductive Technologies of the American Fertility Society 1986, Vol. 46, no. 3. *Fertility and Sterility. Supplement 1 Official Journal of the American Fertility Society.*

Fastvold, Marianne 1977. "Fødselsrett og likhet" (Birth Law and Equality). *Kvinnerettslige studier*, nr. 2. Institute of Women's Law, University of Oslo.

Fastvold, Marianne 1985a. "Rettssikkerhet under fødsel" (Legal Safeguards During Birth). *In* Tove Stang Dahl (ed.), *Kvinnerett I*. Oslo: Universitetsforlaget. *Also in* Anne Hellum (ed.) 1993. *Birth Law*. Oslo: Scandinavian University Press.

Fastvold, Marianne 1985b. "Kvinners arbeid og integritet i familien" (Married Women's Work and Integrity). *In* Tove Stang Dahl (ed.), *Kvinnerett II*. Oslo: Universitetsforlaget. *Also in* Marianne Fastvold & Anne Hellum 1988. *Money and Work in Marriage. Women's Perspectives on Family Law*. Studies in Women's Law no. 26. Institute of Public and International Law Publication Series no. 6, University of Oslo.

Fastvold, Marianne 1990. *Fødsels- og omsorgsrett for foreldre* (Birth Law for Parents). Oslo: Grøndahl.

Fastvold, Marianne & Anne Hellum 1985. *Penger og arbeid i ekteskap – et kvinnesyn på familieretten* (Money and Work in Marriage: Women's Perspectives on Family Law). Institutt for offentlig retts skriftserie nr. 3. Oslo: University of Oslo. *Also in* Marianne Fastvold & Anne Hellum 1988. *Money and Work in Marriage. Women's Perspectives on Family Law*. Studies in Women's Law no. 26. Institute of Public and International Law Publication Series no. 6, University of Oslo.

Firestone, Shulamit 1970. *Kjønnenes dialektikk* (The Dialectic of Sex). Oslo: Gyldendal.

Forest, Gillian C. et al. 1981. "Practical Management of Perinatal Death", *British Medical Journal*, Vol. 282, pp. 31–2.

Forest, Gillian C. et al. "Support after Perinatal Death: A Study of Support and Counselling after Perinatal Bereavement", *British Medical Journal*, Vol. 285, pp. 1475–9.

From One Earth to One World. World Commission on Environment and Development, 1987.

Frost, Lis 1989. "Reproduktionsteknologi: Rettigheds- procedural- eller omsorgsetik?" (The Technology of Reproduction: Legal and Moral Aspects). *Tidsskrift for rettsvitenskap*, nr. 2, pp. 89 f.

Gannik, Houd, Møller, Wolf & Marcusson 1982. *Tolv hjemmefødsler 1980–81, Aktionsforskningsprosjekt i Storstrøms Amt* (Twelve Home Births), Storstrøm Amtskommume, Danmark.

Gilligan, Carol 1982. *In a Different Voice*. Cambridge: Harvard University Press.

Gotaas, Anne-Marit 1980. "Barnefødsel i dølgsmål" (Hidden Births). *In* Gotaas et al. *Det Kriminelle Kjønn*. Oslo: Pax forlag.

Gotaas, Anne-Marit, Brita Gulli, Kari Melby & Aina Schiøtz 1980. *Det Kriminelle Kjønn* (The Criminal Sex). Oslo: Pax forlag.

Grandjean, P. (ed). 1988. *Miljø medisin* (Environmental Medicine). Copenhagen: FADL's Forlag.

Grof, Stanislav 1979. *Den Indre Reise* (The Inner Journey). Copenhagen: Borgen.

Grünfeld, Berthold 1973. *Legal abort i Norge*. (Legal Abortion in Norway). Oslo: Universitetsforlaget.

Grünfeld, Berthold 1976. *Hvem er de umoralske? Om den nye abortloven. Gjengivelse av foredragene på aborthøring arrangert av Brød og Roser*. (Who are the Immoral Ones? The New Abortion Act. Lectures from a Hearing on Abortion). Oslo.

Gulli, Brita 1980. "Abortlovgivningens historie" (History of Abortion Legislation). *In* Gotaas et al. *Det Kriminelle kjønn* (The Criminal Sex). Oslo: Pax forlag.

Gåsvatn, Kari & Bitten Muthe-Kaas 1983. *Foster-diagnostikk til hvilken pris?* (Foetus Diagnosis: At What Price?). Oslo: Cappelen.

Hagemann, Gro 1973. *Særbeskyttelse av kvinner, arbeidvern eller diskriminering?* (Positive Discrimination of Women: Protection or Discrimination?). Thesis in History. Oslo: University of Oslo.

Halsaa, Beatrice & Else Viestad (eds.) 1990. *I pose og sekk. Framtidsbilder* (To Have It Both Ways. Visions for the Future). Oslo: Emilia Press.

Halvorsen, Marit 1985a. "Diskriminering ved ansettelser. Om likstillingslovens §4, annet ledd" (Discrimination in Appointments: Section 4 (2) of the Norwegian Equal Opportunity Act). *In* Tove Stang Dahl (ed.), *Kvinnerett II*. Oslo: Universitetsforlaget.

Halvorsen, Marit 1985b. "Kjønn og lønn" (Sex and Salary: A Study of the Equal Pay Provision of the Norwegian Equal Rights Act). *In* Tove Stang Dahl (ed.), *Kvinnerett II*. Oslo: Universitetsforlaget.

Harding, Sandra 1986. *The Science Question in Feminism*. Ithaca: Cornell University Press.

Harding, Sandra (ed.) 1987. *Feminism and Methodology*. Bloomington: Indiana University Press.

Haukaa, Runa, Marit Hoel & Hanne Haavind (eds.) 1982. *Kvinneforskning: Bidrag til samfunnsteori* (Women's Studies: A Contribution to Social Theory). Oslo: Universitetsforlaget.

Hellum, Anne 1985. "Penger og verdihet etter ektefellelovens §1" (Money and Dignity in Section 1 of the Spouses Property Relationship Act). *In* Tove Stang Dahl (ed.) *Kvinnerett II*. Oslo: Universitetsforlaget. *Also in* Marianne Fastvold & Anne Hellum 1988. *Money and Work in Marriage. Women's Perspectives on Family Law*. Studies in Women's Law, no. 26. Institute of Public and International Law Publication Series no. 6, University of Oslo.

Hellum, Anne 1987. "Morskap, teknologi og rett" (Motherhood, Technology and the Law). *Retfærd*, no. 36.

Hellum, Anne 1990. "Infertilitet og fosterskader i økologisk og rettslig perspektiv" (Infertility and Foetal Disabilities in Ecological and Legal Perspective). *In* Anne Hellum et al. (eds.), *Menneske, natur og fødselsteknologi – Verdivalg og rettslig regulering*. Oslo: Ad Notam forlag.

Hellum, Anne, Aslak Syse & Henriette Sinding Aasen 1990. *Menneske, natur og fødselsteknologi – Verdivalg og rettslig regulering* (Humans, Nature and Birth Technology: Law and Ethics). Oslo: Ad Notam forlag .

Hellum, Anne (ed.) 1993. *Birth Law*. Oslo: Scandinavian University Press.

Hernes, Helga Maria 1982a. *Staten – kvinner ingen adgang* (The State: No Entry for Women). Oslo: Universitetsforlaget.

Hernes, Helga Maria 1982b. "Offentliggjøring av familien" (The Family goes Public). *In* Haukaa et al. (eds.), *Kvinneforskning: Bidrag til samfunnsteori*. Oslo: Universitetsforlaget.

Hernes, Helga Maria 1987. *Welfare State and Woman Power*. Oslo: Norwegian University Press.

Hodne, Bjarne 1980. *Å leve med døden* (Living with Death). Oslo: Aschehoug.

Hubbard, Ruth 1986. "Eugenics and Prenatal Testing", *International Journal of Health Services*, Vol. 16, no. 2.
Huxley, Aldous 1985. Vidunderlige nye verden (Brave New World). Oslo: Aschehoug.
Huxley, Julian 1931. "The Vital Importance of Eugenics", *Harper's Magazine*.
Høigård, Cecilie 1983. "Kvinnelige lovbrytere" (Female Offenders). *In* Høigård & Snare (eds), *Kvinners skyld*. Oslo: Pax forlag.
Høigård, Cecilie & Annika Snare 1983. *Kvinners skyld* (Women's Guilt: An Anthology). Oslo: Pax forlag.
Haavind, Hanne 1989. "Rasjonalitet, makt og følelser" (Rationality, Power and Emotions). *Nytt Norsk Tidsskrift*, nr. 3.
Illich, Ivan 1977. *Teknologi for jamvektssamfunnet* (Tools for Conviviality). Oslo: Pax forlag.
Jaggar, Alison m.fl. 1983. *Feminist Politics and Human Nature*. Sussex: The Harvester Press.
Johnsen, Marianne E. 1989. *Bibliografi i fødselsrett* (Bibliography of Birth Law). Kvinnerettslige Arbeidsnotater nr. 42. Institute of Women's Law, University of Oslo.
Johnsen, Marianne E. 1990. *Fosterets rettsstilling: Er det styrket – Bør det styrkes?* (The Legal Status of the Foetus: Is it Strengthened. Should It Be Strengthened?). Thesis in Law. Kvinnerettslige arbeidsnotater nr. 43. Institute of Women's Law, University of Oslo.
Kaufmann, Caroline 1988. "Perfect Mothers, Perfect Babies: An Examination of Fetal Treatment", *Reproductive and Genetic Engineering*, Vol. 1, no. 2.
Kaul, Hjørdis 1990. "Who Cares? Gender, Inequality and Care Leave in the Nordic Countries", *Acta Sociologica*.
Keller, Evelyn Fox 1985. *Reflections on Gender and Science*. New Haven: Yale University Press.
Ketscher, Kirsten 1986. "Mænd har ikke råd til barselsorlov" (Men Cannot Afford Birth Leave). Copenhagen: *Årsberetning for Retsvitenskabligt Institut B*.
Ketscher, Kirsten 1989. "Familieretten i opløsning" (Family Law in Dissolution). Copenhagen: *Samkvind Skriftserie*, nr. 2.
Ketscher, Kirsten 1990. *Offentlig børnepasning i retlig belysning* (Public Child Care in a Legal Perspective). Copenhagen: Jurist og Økonomforbundets Forlag.
Kishwar, Madhu 1985. "The Continuing Deficit of Women in India and the Impact of Amniocentesis", in G. Corea (ed.), *Man-Made Women*. London: Hutchinson.
Kjønstad, Asbjørn 1982. "Pasienters rettigheter – kontraktsrett eller forvaltningsrett?" (Patients' Rights: Contract Law or Administrative Law?). *In*: *Lov og frihet: Festskrift til Johs Andenæs*. Oslo: Universitetsforlaget.
Kjønstad, Asbjørn (ed.) 1984. *Folketrygden i støpeskjeen* (Changing Prospects for the National Insurance System). Oslo: Universitetsforlaget.
Koch, Lene 1987. "Towards a Feminist Assessment of Reproductive Technology", *Acta Sociologica*, no. 2.
Kolder, V. E. B., J. Gallagher & M. Parsons 1987. "Court Ordered Obstetrical Interventions", *The New England Journal of Medicine*, Vol. 326, no. 19.
Kvisli, Kari og Informasjonsutvalget for funksjonshemmede 1983. *Det er noe i veien med barnet* (There is Something Wrong with the Child). Oslo 2 utg.
Leuzinger, Monika & Bigna Rambert 1988. "I Can Feel If My Baby is Healthy: Women's Experiences with Prenatal Diagnosis in Switzerland", *Reproductive and Genetic Engineering*, Vol. 1, no. 3.
Lewis, Emanuel 1979. "Mourning by the Family after a Stillbirth or Neonatal Death", *Archives of Disease in Childhood*, Vol. 54, pp. 303–6.
Lindberg, Bo 1983. "Föräldrareaktioner ved perinatal död" (Parents' Reactions after Perinatal Death). *Jordmodern*, Vol. 96, pp. 5–14.
Mies, Maria 1986. *Patriarchy and Accumulation on a World Scale*. London: Zed Books Ltd.

Mohr, Tone 1969. *Katti Anker Møller – en banebryter* (Katti Anker Møller – a Pioneer). Oslo: Tiden.

Møller, Katti Anker 1974. Moderskabets Frigjørelse. To foredrag fra 1915 og 1919. (The Liberation of Motherhood. Two lectures from 1915 and 1919). Oslo: Tiden norsk forlag.

Munthe-Kaas, Bitten 1985. *Når barnet dør før livet begynner* (When a Child Dies Before Life Starts). Oslo.

Nielsen, Ruth 1978. *Kvindesarbejdsret* (Women's Labour Law). Copenhagen: Juristforbundets Forlag.

Nielsen, Ruth 1986. *Ledelsesrett og ligestilling. En komparativ arbejdsretlig analyse* (The Politics of Equality and the Employer's Rights). Copenhagen: Jurist- og Økonomforbundes Forlag.

Nilsson, Dag 1980. "Fødeavdelingens rutiner ved dødfødsel" (Maternity Ward Routines in Connection with Stillbirths). *Tidsskrift for Den norske Lægeforening*, pp. 1619 f.

Nittert, Irmgard 1988. *Die Geburt von ein behindertes Kind* (The Birth of a Handicapped Child). Ferdinand Enke Verlag.

Noddings, Nel 1984. *Caring: A Feminine Approach to Ethics and Moral Education.* Berkeley: University of California Press.

Nordborg, Gudrun 1987. "Reproduktionsteknologi och rashygien" (Reproduction Technology and Racial Hygiene). *Retfærd*, nr. 38.

Oakley, Ann 1984. *The Captured Womb: A History of the Medical Care of Pregnant Women*. Oxford: Basil Blackwell.

O'Brien, Mary 1981. *The Politics of Reproduction.* London: Routledge & Kegan Paul.

Olsen, Frances 1988. "Forældremyndighed og reproduktionsteknologi. En kommentar til Baby-M sagen" (Parental Rights and Reproduction Technology: A Response to the Baby M Case). *Retfærd*, nr. 42.

Olsnes, Ragnhild 1985. "Retten til sjølbestemt abort" (The Right to Self-determined Abortion). *In* Tove Stang Dahl (ed.), *Kvinnerett II.* Oslo: Universitetsforlaget. *Also in* Anne Hellum (ed.) 1993. *Birth Law* Oslo: Scandinavian University Press.

Osser, S., P. Liedholm & J. Ranstam 1984. "Depressed Semen Quality: A Study Over Two Decades," *Archives of Andryology*, Vol. 12, pp. 113–6.

Parmann, Øistein 1989. "De usedvanlige menneskene" (Extraordinary People). *Aftenposten*, 15th December.

Pateman, Carole & Elisabeth Gross (eds.) *Feminist Challenges: Social and Political Theory*. Boston: Northeastern University Press.

Pedersen, Gøril 1989. *Litteraturoversikt i internasjonal fødselsrett* (Bibliographical Survey of International Birth Law). Kvinnerettslige Arbeidsnotater nr. 37. Institute of Women's Law, University of Oslo.

Peppers, Larry G. & Ronald J. Knapp 1980. "Maternal Reactions to Involuntary Fetal/Infant Death", *Psychiatry*, Vol. 43, pp. 155–9.

Pentikäinen, Juha 1968. *The Nordic Death-Child Tradition.* Helsinki.

Petersen, Hanne 1987. *Ledelse og loyaltitet. Kollektiv arbejdsret i den offentlige sektor* (Management and Loyalty: Labour Law in the Public Sector). Copenhagen: Akademisk Forlag.

Petersen, Hanne 1990. *Informel ret og hensynsnorm på kvindearbejdspladser* (Informal Law in Women's Work Places). Copenhagen: Akademisk Forlag.

Report of the Committee of Inquiry into Human Fertilisation and Embryology 1984. Department of Health and Social Security. London

Rich, Adrienne 1977. *Of Woman Born: Motherhood as Experience and Institution.* New York: Bantam Books.

Robertson, John A. 1983. "Procreative Liberty and the Control of Conception, Pregnancy and Childbirth", *Virginia Law Review*, Vol. 69, no. 3.

Roggenkamp, Viola 1984. "Abortion of a Special Kind: Male Sex Selection in India." *In* Rita Arditti et al. (eds), *Test-tube Women: What Future for Motherhood?* London: Pandora Press.
Royal College of Physicians of London 1989. *Prenatal Diagnosis and Genetic Screening*. London.
Ryall, Anka 1990. "Se for dere et sammenfiltret kratt. Alternative bilder i Charles Darwins Om artenes opprinnelse (Imagine a Tangled Thicket: Utopias in Charles Darwin's On the Origin of the Species). *In* Beatrice Halsaa & Else Viestad (eds.), *I pose og sekk*. Oslo: Emilia Press
Saba A/S 1978. *Graviditet, fødsel og spedbarnstell. Håndbok for foreldre* (Pregnancy, Birth and the Care of Newborn Babies: Handbook for Parents).Tønsberg.
Sajo, A. (ed.) 1989. *High-Technology and Law: A Critical Approach*. Budapest: Institute of Political and Legal Sciences.
Salvesen, Kjell et al. 1990. "Prenatal diagnostikk og Down's syndrom" (Prenatal Diagnosis and Down's Syndrome). *Tidsskrift for Den norske Lægeforening*, nr. 6.
Sandberg, Kirsten 1990. *Barnets beste. Om barnefordeling, rettspraksis og rettferdighet* (In the Best Interests of the Child: Custody, Court Practice and Justice). Oslo: Ad Notam forlag.
Schenker, J. G. & D. Weinstein 1986. "The Intra-Uterine Life, Management and Therapy", *Excerpta Medica*.
Shiva, Vandana 1989. *Til livets opphold. Kvinner Økologi og utvikling* (Staying Alive: Women, Ecology and Development). Oslo: Oktober.
Skjeie, Hege 1982. *Den som lo først, LO best.* (The National Federation of Labour and the Equal Status Act). Thesis in Political Science. University of Oslo.
Sjøgren, Berit & Nils Uddenberg 1988. "Decision-making During the Prenatal Diagnostic Procedure: A Questionnaire and Interview Study of 211 Women Participating in Prenatal Diagnosis", *Prenatal Diagnosis*, Vol. 8.
Smith, Dorothy E. 1987. *The Everyday World as Problematic: A Feminist Sociology*. Boston: Northeastern University Press.
Smith, Lucy 1980. *Foreldremyndighet og barnerett* (Parental Rights and Child Law). Oslo: Universitetsforlaget.
Smith, Peder Hersleb 1823. *Kongelige Forordninger og Aabne Breve 1670–1814* (Royal Ordinances and Open Letters 1670–1814). Christiania.
Stabel, Ingse 1988. "Rett og teknologi- eksemplet fødselsteknologi" (Law and Technology: The Case of Birth Technology). *Retfærd*, nr. 43.
Standish, Liz 1982. "The Loss of a Baby", *The Lancet*, pp. 611–2.
Statistisk ukehefte nr. 12 1982, Statistisk Sentralbyrå (Weekly Statistics no. 12. Central Bureau of Statistics). Oslo.
Sverdrup, Tone 1984. "Folketrygden i kvinneperspectiv" (Social Security from Women's Perspective). *In* A. Kjønstad (ed.), *Folketrygden i støpeskjeen*. Oslo: Universitetsforlaget.
Sverdrup, Tone 1985. "Det to-sporede lovsystemet – belyst med eksempler fra skatteretten" (The Two Track Legal System: Illustrated by examples from Tax Law). *In* Tove Stang Dahl (ed.), *Kvinnerett II*. Oslo: Universitetsforlaget.
Syse, Aslak 1990. "Fra egg til menneske – medisinske og rettslige problemstillinger knyttet til fosterets utvikling" (From Ovum to Human Being: Medical and Legal Consequences Associated with Foetal Development). *In* Anne Hellum et al. (eds.), *Menneske, natur og fødselsteknologi – Verdivalg og rettslig regulering*. Oslo: Ad Notam forlag.
Tranøy, Knut Erik 1989. "Den nye fruktbarhetsteknologien – nye og gamle rettigheter" (The New Fertility Technology: New and Old Rights). *Tidsskrift for rettvitenskap*, nr. 2, pp. 122 f.
Tymstra, Tjeerd 1989. *The Imperative Character of Medical Technology and the Meaning of Anticipated Decision Regret*. Cambridge: Cambridge University Press.
Ulstein, Magnar, et al. 1990. "Svangerskapsutfall i noen norske fylker før og etter Tsjernobyl ulykken" (The Outcome of Pregnancies in some Norwegian Counties

before and after the Chernobyl Accident). *Tidsskrift for Den norske Lægeforening*, nr. 3, pp. 359–62.

Ve, Hildur 1990. "Kvinners kunnskap – forutsening for en alternativ fremtid?" (Women's Knowledge – Preconditions for an Alternative Future). *In* Halsaa and Viestad (eds.), *I pose og sekk*. Oslo: Emilia Press.

Waring, Marilyn 1988. *If Women Counted: A New Feminist Economics*. New York: Harper & Row.

Warnock, M. 1985. *A Question of Life: The Warnock Report on Human Fertilisation and Embryology*. New York: Basil Blackwell.

Wesenberg, Jane 1990. *Utuktig handling og atferd. Straffelovens §212* (A Feminist Study of Supreme Court Practice in Cases of Breach of Penal Code §212 on Offences against Modesty by Obscene Conduct and Indecent Acts Against Children under 16 years of age). Thesis in Law. Institute of Women's Law, University of Oslo.

Widerberg, Karin 1984. "Världens bästa reformer? Den svenska föräldraledighetlagsstiftningen och verkeligheten" (The World's Best Reforms? The Reality Behind the Swedish Rules on Parents' Leave of Absence during Children's Sickness). *Jussens Venner*, nr. 6–7.

Widerberg, Karin 1985. "Försörjing i ett könskampperspektiv" (Maintenance in a Gender Perspective). *Retfærd*, nr. 28.

Wikan, Unni 1989. "Towards an Experience-near Anthropology", Plenary Speech for the Society for Cultural Anthropology Meetings. Washington D.C.

Wretmark, Astrid Andersson 1979. "Det tidligt döda barnet och den förtigna sorgen" (Death of the Newborn Baby and the Suppressed Grief). *Läkartidningen*, nr. 76, pp. 4643 f.

Wretmark, Astrid Andersson 1980. "Dödan innan livet riktigt har börjat" (Death Before Life has Really Started). *Läkartidningen*, nr. 77, pp. 4042 f.

Ysen, Heidi 1989. *Utuktig omgang med mindreårige. Straffelovens §195 og §196 i Høyesterett 1960–1986* (Indecent Relations with Minors: Supreme Court Practice on Sections 195 and 196 of the Penal Code from 1960 to 1986). Thesis in law. Kvinnerettslige Arbeidsnotater nr. 38. Institute of Women's Law, University of Oslo.

Aanesen, Ellen 1981. *Ikke send meg til en kone, doktor!* (Don't Send Me to a Sourcerer, Doctor). Oslo: Oktober.

Aasen, Henriette Sinding 1989. *Rasehygiene og menneskeverd. Nasjonalsosialismens steriliseringslov av 23 juli 1942.* (Race Hygiene and Human Worth. The National Socialist Act on Sterilisation of 23rd July 1942). Kvinnerettslige studier nr. 28. Institutt for offentlig retts skriftserie nr. 4, University of Oslo.

Aasen, Henriette Sinding 1990a. "Noen historiske perspektiver knytlet til dagens utvikling innen prenatal diagnostikk" (An Historical Perspective on Current Developments within Prenatal Diagnostics). *In* Anne Hellum et al. (eds.) *Menneske, natur og fødselsteknologi – Verdivalg og rettslig regulering*. Oslo: Ad Notam forlag.

Aasen, Henriette Sinding 1990b. "Hva slags barn? Abortdebatt med nytt innhold" (What Kind of Children. A New Content to the Debate on Abortion). *Retfærd*, nr. 50. *Also in* Anne Hellum (ed.) 1993. *Birth Law*. Oslo: Scandinavian University Press.

Aasen, Henriette Sinding 1991. "Fosterdiagnostik och rätten att välja" (Foetal Diagnostics and the Right to Choose), *Kvinnevitenskapelig Tidsskrift*, nr. 1.

Scandinavian Travaux Préparatoires and other Public Reports

Denmark

Fremskridtets Pris, Indenrigsministeriet 1984, København (The Price of Progress, Danish Home Office 1984, Copenhagen).

NU B 1979:10 Barselsorlov – forældre og børns behov i perioden omkring graviditet, fødsel og barnets første leveår, spesielt med henblik på barselsorlov. (Danish Official Reports No. 10 for 1979: Maternity Leave – The Special Needs of Parents and Children During Pregnancy, Birth and the Child's First Year, particularly with regard to Maternity Leave).

NU A 1980: Fødselsinstitusjoner i Norden (Birth Institutions in Scandinavia).

Norway

Innst.O.nr. 47 1974–75 *Innstilling fra sosialkomiteen om lov om svangerskapsavbrudd* (Recommendation to the Odelsting No. 47 for 1974- 75. Recommendation from the Parliamentary Committee on Social Affairs relating to the Abortion Act).

NAVF 1988. *Handling gjennom kunnskap*. Rapport til NAVF's styre fra ad hoc-utvalget for oppfølging av Verdenskommisjonens rapport om miljø og utvikling (Action Through Knowledge. Report to the Board of the Norwegian Research Council for Science and the Humanities (NAVF) from the Ad-hoc Committee appointed to follow up the Report from the World Commission on Environment and Development).

NOU 1977:35 *Lov om barn og foreldre (barneloven)* (Norwegian Official Reports No. 35 for 1977: The Act relating to Children and Parents (The Children Act)).

NOU 1984:17 *Perinatal omsorg i Norge. Helsearbeid blant svangre og fødende kvinner samt nyfødte barn* (Norwegian Official Reports No. 17 for 1984: Perinatal Care in Norway. Health Care Amongst Pregnant Women and Newborn Children).

NOU 1984:30 *Pleie og omsorg for alvorlige syke og døende mennesker* (Norwegian Official Reports No. 30 for 1984: Nursing and Care of Seriously Ill and Dying Persons).

Ot.prp.nr. 15 (1959) *Om lov om adgang til å avbryte svangerskap* (Proposition to the Odelsting No. 15 for 1959: The Act relating to the Right to Terminate Pregnancy).

Ot.prp.nr. 38 (1974–75) *Om lov om svangerskapsavbrudd* (Proposition to the Odelsting No. 38 for 1974–75: Act concerning Termination of Pregnancy).

Ot.prp.nr. 53 (1977–78) *Om lov om endring i lov av 13. juni 1975 nr. 50 om svangerskapsavbrudd* (Proposition to the Odelsting No. 53 for 1977–78: The Act relating to the Amendment of the Abortion Act of 13th June 1975, No. 50).

Ot.prp.nr. 1 (1979–80) *Om lov om leger og lov om tannleger, med NOU 1976: 1 Legers og tannlegers rettigheter og plikter* (Proposition to the Odelsting No. 1 for 1979–80 on the Act relating to Medical Practitioners and the Act relating to Dentists, with Norwegian Official Reports No. 1 for 1976: The Rights and Duties of Medical Practitioners and Dentists).

Ot.prp.nr. 62 (1979–80) *Om lov om barn og foreldre (barneloven) med NOU 1977:35 Lov om barn og foreldre (barneloven)* (Proposition to the Odelsting No. 62 for

1979–80 on the Act relating to Children and Parents (The Children Act), with Norwegian Official Reports No. 35 for 1977: The Act relating to Children and Parents (The Children Act)).

Ot.prp.nr. 25 (1988–87) *Om lov om kunstig befruktning, Sosialdepartementet Oslo* (Proposition to the Odelsting No. 25 for 1986–87: The Act relating to Artificial Procreation, Ministry of Social Affairs, Oslo).

Sosialdepartementet (Ministry of Social Affairs) 1978. *Amming i Norge* (Breastfeeding in Norway). Oslo.

Sosialdepartementet: *Lov om svangerskapsavbrudd med endringer, forskrifter og veiledning (I–2062)* (Ministry of Social Affairs: The Abortion Act with Amendments, Regulations and Orienteering).

St. forh. 1974–75 *Debatter m.v. i Odelstinget p. 377–446* (Proceedings in the Storting 1974–75: Debates etc. in the Odelsting pp. 377–446).

St.meld. no. 9 (1974–75) se s.33.

St.meld.nr. 51 (1973–74) *Barnefamiliens levekår* (Report to the Storting No. 51 for 1973–74: The Standard of Living of Families with Children).

St.meld.nr. 32 (1976–77) *Rettssikkerhet i sosial- og helseinstitusjoner* (Report to the Storting No. 32 for 1976–77: Legal Safeguards in Social and Public Health Institutions).

St.meld.nr. 73 (1981–82) *Om organisering av medisinsk-genetiske servicefunksjoner i Norge* (Report to the Storting No. 73 for 1981–82: The Organisation of Medico-Genetical Services in Norway).

St.meld.nr. 17 (1982–83) *Erfaringer med lov om svangerskapsavbrudd og svangerskapsforebyggende tiltak* (Report to the Storting No. 17 for 1982–83: Experiences with the Termination of Pregnancy Act, and Measures to Prevent Pregnancy).

St.meld.nr. 46 (1988–89) *Miljø og utvikling. Norges oppfølging av Verdenskommisjonens rapport* (Report to the Storting No. 46 for 1988–89: Environment and Development. Norway's follow-up of the World Commission's Report).

Straffelovkomiteens innstilling nr. 1, 1935. *Angående forandring i straffeloven §245 og angående utferdigelse av lov om avbrytelse av svangerskap* (First Recommendation of the Criminal Law Commission relating to Amendments to Section 245 of The Penal Code, and relating to the Implementation of an Act Relating to Termination of Pregnancy).

Straffelovrådets innstilling 1956. *Om adgang til avbrytelse av svangerskap* (Recommendation of the Criminal Law Commission relating to the Right to Termination of Pregnancy).

Sweden

Jordmoderarbejde, Storstrøm Amtskommune, Social- og Sundhetsforvaltningen, Descmber 1978 (The Work of Midwives, Storstrøm Local Authority, Administration for Health and Social Affairs, December 1978).

SOU 1989. *Den gravida kvinnan och fostret två individer. Om foster diagnostikk. Om sena aborter* (Swedish Official Reports 1989: The Pregnant Woman and the Foetus: Two Individuals. About Diagnostics and Foetal Terminations During the Later Stages of Pregnancy). Stockholm.

Statutes

Denmark's and Norway's Church Ritual of 1685.
The Norwegian Laws of King Christian the Fifth of 1687.
The Constitution of the Kingdom of Norway, 17 May 1814 (The Constitution).
The Act relating to Churches and Churchyards, 3 August 1897, No. 1 (The Churches and Churchyards Act).
The Penal Code, 22 May 1902, No. 10 (The Penal Code).
The Act relating to the Property Relationship between the Spouses, 2 May 1927, No. 1 (The Spouses Property Relationship Act).
The Act for the Protection of the National Lineage, 23 July 1942, No. 1.
The Child Allowance Act, 24 October 1946, No. 2 (The Child Allowance Act).
The Child Welfare Act, 17 July 1953, No. 14 (The Child Welfare Act).
The Mental Health Act, 28 April 1961, No. 2.
The Act concerning Termination of Pregnancy in Certain Cases of 11 November 1960, No. 2.
The Personal Names Act, 29 May 1964, No. 3 (The Names Act).
The National Insurance Act, 17 June 1966, No. 12 (The National Insurance Act).
The Act relating to Public Administration, 10 February 1967, No. 55 (The Public Administration Act).
The Act on Hospitals etc., 19 June 1969, No. 57 (The Hospitals Act).
The Nature Conservation Act, 19 June 1970, No. 63 (The Nature Conservation Act).
The Nuclear Energy Act, 12 May 1972, No. 28 (The Nuclear Energy Act).
The Act relating to Allodial Matters, 28 June 1974, No. 58.
The Termination of Pregnancy Act, 13 June 1975, No. 50 (The Abortion Act).
The Working Environment Act, 4 February 1977, No. 4 (The Working Environment Act).
The Sterilization Act, 3 June 1977, No. 57 (The Sterilization Act).
The Act relating to Equal Status Between the Sexes, 9 June 1978, No. 45 (The Equal Status Act).
The Act relating to Medical Practitioners, 13 June 1980, No. 42 (The Medical Practitioners Act).
The Act relating to Pollution Control, 13 March 1981, No. 6 (The Pollution Control Act).
The Act relating to Children and Parents, 8 April 1981, No. 7 (The Children Act).
The Act relating to Municipal Health Services, 19 November 1982, No. 66 (The Municipal Health Services Act).
The Midwives Act, 26 April 1985, No. 23 (The Midwives Act).
The Act relating to Adoption, 28 February 1986, No. 8 (The Adoption Act).
The Act relating to Artificial Procreation, 12 June 1987, No. 68 (The Artificial Procreation Act).
The Act relating to Maintenance in Advance, 17 February 1989, No. 2.

Contributors

KIRSTI STRØM BULL, born 1945, graduated from the Faculty of Law, University of Oslo in 1969, served as a deputy judge 1970–71, and since 1981 has been senior lecturer at the Institute of Private Law at the University of Oslo. She has published a number of articles on family law, tort law and women's law. She is editor of the anthology *Skilsmisse* (Divorce) (Gyldendal, 1982) and author of *Ugift Samliv* (Unmarried Cohabitation) (Tano, 1990).

TOVE STANG DAHL, born 1938, graduated from the Faculty of Law, University of Oslo in 1964, and was awarded Dr. philos. (Doctor of Science) for her thesis *Child Welfare and Social Defence* (Norwegian University Press, 1985) in 1978. She has held the posts of lecturer at the Institute of Criminology and Criminal Law, Senior Lecturer at the Institute of Public and International Law and Professor of Women's Law at the Faculty of Law at the University of Oslo. Since 1975 she has been the academic head of the Department of Women's Law. She is the author of *Women's Law. An Introduction to Feminist Jurisprudence* (Norwegian University Press, 1985) *Den muslimske familie* (The Muslim Family/ Universitetsforlaget 1992) and has published a number of articles and anthologies on criminology, legal sociology, social law and women's law.

MARIANNE FASTVOLD, born 1951, graduated from the Faculty of Law, University of Oslo in 1979. She has been a researcher at the Department of Women's Law and is now researcher for the organization Alternativ Framtid (Alternative Future). She has published mainly in the field of birth law and housewives' law. Along with Anne Hellum she is author of *Money and Work in Marriage*. Women's Perspectives on Family Law (Studies in Women's Law) (University of Oslo, 1988). She is author of *Fødsels- og omsorgsrett for foreldre* (Birth and Care Law for Parents) (Grøndahl, 1990). In 1992, she made her debut as a fiction writer with the collection of short stories *Dame i Svev* (Woman in Flight) (Gyldendal, 1992).

ANNE HELLUM, born 1952, graduated from the Faculty of Law, University of Oslo in 1980, and was awarded an intermediary degree in social anthropology in 1986. She has been a researcher at the Department of Women's Law at the University of Oslo and course leader for the NORAD Diploma Course in Women's Law, a post-graduate education programme for female lawyers from southern and eastern Africa. She has also served as a deputy judge. She has published in the field of women's law and development law, and is co-editor of the anthology *Menneske, natur og fødselsteknologi* (Humans, Nature and Reproduction Technology) (Ad Notam, 1990); along with Marianne Fastvold she is co-author of *Money and Work in Marriage* (University of Oslo, 1988).

RAGNHILD OLSNES, born 1958, graduated from the Faculty of Law, University of Oslo in 1984. She has been an executive officer at the Ministry of Petroleum and Energy and has worked in private practice as an associate lawyer and in her own practice. She now works at the Department of Women's Law, researching in the field of legal education and legal assistance in the third world. She has published a number of legal political articles in Scandinavian journals.

HENRIETTE SINDING AASEN, born 1963, graduated from the Faculty of Law, University of Oslo in 1989. She has been a researcher at the Department of Women's Law at the University of Oslo, and since 1991 has been a research fellow at the University of Bergen, sponsored by the Norwegian Research Council for Science and the Humanities. She has published a number of articles in the field of eugenics and reproduction control, and is co-editor of the anthology *Menneske, natur og fødselsteknologi* (Humans, Nature and Reproduction Technology) (Ad Notam, 1990).